# Powerhouse

## An Upper Intermediate Business English Course

**David Evans**

**with Grammar Reference
by Peter Strutt**

Longman

# 1 first impressions

**FORMING AN IMPRESSION**

*Sigourney Weaver as Katherine in Working Girl*

Work in small groups and discuss these questions.

1 When you form a first impression of someone, which of these is most important to you? Rank them from 1 (most important) to 5 (least important).

> the way they look at you
> the way they dress
> the way they speak
> their job or who they work for
> the way they shake your hand or greet you

2 What other things are important when you form a first impression? Think of at least two.

**DESCRIBING IMPRESSIONS**

Work in pairs and answer these questions.

1 Which of the adjectives in the box would normally describe people in the following?

> simple
> accommodating
> tough
> accurate
> elegant
> punctual
> impeccable

▌ their dealings with others
▌ their approach to their work
▌ their appearance

2 Which of these adjectives describe the kind of impression that you'd like to create in your business life? Think of two other adjectives that describe the kind of image that you'd like to have.

**WORKING GIRL**

*Working Girl* is a movie set in a Wall Street investment bank. In the scene opposite, the new boss, Katherine (Sigourney Weaver), calls her assistant, Tess (Melanie Griffith), into her office for their first meeting.

*Tess at the start of the movie*

**THE SCRIPT**  Read the script at the bottom of the page and answer these questions.

1 What qualities does Katherine expect Tess to have?
2 How does she think that Tess should dress?
3 What's her opinion of the way that their department has performed in the past?

**KATHERINE'S LANGUAGE**  Look again at the script and answer these questions.

1 What do you think that Katherine means by these four phrases?

▌ People's impression of me starts with you.
▌ I'm never on another line, I'm in a meeting.
▌ I want your input, Tess.
▌ It's a two-way street on my team.

2 Why do you think she says 'call me Katherine'?

**DRESS CODE**  Look again at the saying of Coco Chanel that Katherine quotes and then talk about these questions.

1 Do you think that Coco Chanel's idea about the way that women should dress also applies to men?
2 Does her idea apply to all areas of business? (Think about industries such as advertising, engineering and software development.)

**WORKING GIRL AND YOU**

**1**  Is Katherine the kind of person that you'd like to have as your next boss? Explain why or why not.

**2**  Katherine is very clear about the way that a businessperson should behave. In what ways are your ideas different?

---

KATH  So, Tess, a few ground rules. The way I look at it, you are my link with the outside world. People's impression of me starts with you. You're tough when it's warranted, accommodating when you can be. You're accurate, you're punctual and you never make a promise that you can't keep. I'm never on another line, I'm in a meeting. I consider us a team, Tess, and as such, we have a uniform – simple, elegant, impeccable. 'Dress shabbily, they notice the dress; dress impeccably, they notice the woman.' Coco Chanel.

TESS  And how do I look?

KATH  You look terrific. You might want to rethink the jewellery. I want your input, Tess. I welcome your ideas and I like to see hard work rewarded. It's a two-way street on my team. Am I making myself clear?

TESS  Yes, Katherine.

KATH  And call me Katherine.

TESS  OK.

KATH  So, let's get to work, shall we? This department's profile last year was damn pitiful. Our team has got its work cut out for it. Thanks.

▌ **GLOSSARY** ▌

when it's warranted  *when it's necessary*
shabbily  *in poor quality clothes*
Coco Chanel  *famous French fashion designer and businesswoman*
profile  *public image*
damn pitiful  *extremely bad*
to have your work cut out  *to have a lot to do*

*Tess's new look*

## G R A M M A R   R E V I E W

**WHAT'S YOUR IMPRESSION?**

These three businesspeople have all been in the newspaper headlines for one reason or another over the past few years.

What's your impression of these people? Talk about these questions and others that seem relevant.

What kind of jobs do they do?
What are they doing at the moment?
Do they look honest?
What kind of clothes are they wearing?
Do they seem successful?

UNCONVENTIONAL WISDOM

### CHECK

When talking about your impressions, you will probably use either present simple or present continuous tenses.

We use the **present continuous** to talk about a temporary situation or something that's happening now.

*She's **wearing** a blue dress.*

We use the **present simple** to talk about regular actions or normal situations.

*He always **carries** a brown briefcase.*

We also use the present simple with verbs of perception, possession, emotion and belief.

*He **seems** like a nice man.*

❚ *For more on these points, turn to page 143.* ❚

**PRESENT SIMPLE OR CONTINUOUS?**

Check that you remember the use of these tenses by putting the verbs in brackets into the present simple or present continuous form.

*1* She (seem) _____ like a nice woman, but I (not trust) _____ her.
*2* He always (listen) _____ carefully to what his customers (want) _____.
*3* She (sound) _____ convincing but she (not know) _____ what she (talk) _____ about.
*4* He (look) _____ great today because he (wear) _____ his smartest suit.
*5* Everybody (like) _____ his image – that's why his business (grow) _____ so fast at the moment.
*6* Every time he (open) _____ his mouth, he (say) _____ something stupid.
*7* We (try) _____ to raise some more money at the moment, but people (not have) _____ confidence in small businesses.
*8* The dealers (panic) _____ because the market (fall) _____ dramatically this morning.
*9* She (own) _____ five companies but she never (boast) _____ about it.
*10* He (not hide) _____ under the desk – he (look) _____ for his pen!

# *Present and past*

**WHO ARE THEY?**   🔊 👥 Listen to the stories of the three people pictured opposite and do the following.

*1*   Match a name to each of the photos.

> Darius Guppy     Michael Milken     Nicola Horlick

*2*   Why is each one famous?

*3*   How correct were your impressions?

---

| **CHECK** |
| --- |

The stories on the recording use three ways to talk about the past.

| The **past simple** is used for completed actions in the past. | The **past continuous** is used to talk about something that was in progress at a certain time in the past. | ***used to*** describes a normal or regular situation which existed in the past but doesn't exist any more. |
| --- | --- | --- |
| *He invented the junk bond market.* | *He was working in New York when a man threatened him with a gun.* | *He used to be a part of high society.* |

▌ *For more on these points, turn to page 140.* ▌

---

**PAST PRACTICE**   Use these notes to re-tell the three stories, using the appropriate past structures. This is a possible beginning for the first story.

> *Michael Milken used to be the hero of the world's financial markets. He invented the junk bond market and made a fortune from it. He earned ...*

Michael Milken / hero of the world's financial markets / invent junk bond market / make a fortune / earn $550 million in one year
Enemies believe Milken not make money honestly / long investigation / Nov 90 prison for ten years
Prison – Milken changes: before – wear false hair piece / after – completely bald!

Darius Guppy / be part of British high society / wealthy family, Oxford University, friend of Earl Spencer
Lloyd's insurance market – problems / Guppy's family ruined / Guppy – business career
Small company / gems and precious stones
Work in New York / £2 million robbery / insurance claim
Police investigation / March 1993 / five years in prison for fraud

Nicola Horlick / superwoman / top fund manager / responsible for £18 billion / earn over £1 million / married / five children
1996 Deutsche Morgan Grenfell suspend her / Horlick furious / bank act unfairly / PR consultant / to Frankfurt
Leave Deutsche Morgan Grenfell, but now famous / new job as fund manager with another bank / superwoman of British business life again

## *Business jargon*

**IMPLEMENT OR DO?**      The business guru, Peter Drucker, said this about the language that businesspeople sometimes use.

> *The moment people talk of 'implementing' instead of 'doing', and of 'finalising' instead of 'finishing', the organisation is already running a fever.*

▌ **GLOSSARY** ▌

to run a fever   *to suffer from an illness*

What point do you think that Drucker is trying to make?

**DOGBERT'S**      Scott Adams' cartoon characters Dogbert and Dilbert star in the world's most popular satire
**MANAGEMENT**   on modern business life. Look at the cartoons and answer these questions.
**SEMINAR**
*1*  What does Scott Adams think about business jargon?
*2*  Do you think that Peter Drucker would agree with him?

▌ **GLOSSARY** ▌

zombies   *creatures in horror movies
                which seem to be neither living nor dead*
jargon-spewing   *jargon-talking*

**JARGON WORDS**

**1** Which of these jargon words do you recognise? Do you know what any of them mean? (If you're really curious, look them up in a dictionary!)

*paradigm* **utilize** vertical **proactive** *empowerment*

**2** How would you say this sentence in more conventional English?

> I WANT TO DIALOGUE
> WITH YOU ABOUT
> UTILIZING RESOURCES.

**JARGON AND DEFINITIONS**

Here are five of the most common pieces of business jargon of the past few years. All of them describe influential business ideas. Look at the jargon words and their definitions and answer the questions below.

**business process re-engineering** is when a business tries to improve its performance in every area by completely redesigning systems and processes rather than just by changing existing ones.

**management by walking about (MBWA)** is the idea that managers can manage in the best way by visiting places where operations are carried out and by talking to employees.

**empowerment** is when workers in a company are given more responsibility by being allowed to organise their own work and make decisions without asking their managers.

**a portfolio worker** is a professional person who works for many different companies or individuals.

**total quality management** is the management of systems in a company to make sure that each department is working in the most effective way to improve the quality of goods produced or services provided.

*Longman Business English Dictionary*

*1* Which idea is all about getting products and services right first time, rather than checking them for errors when they're finished?

*2* Which idea tells companies to take a blank piece of paper and imagine that they're starting their business all over again?

*3* Which idea makes managers less powerful?

*4* Which idea tells managers to get out of their offices?

*5* Which idea describes people who are independent and run their own careers?

**JARGON AND YOU**

Discuss these questions.

*1* Do you think that the terms above are useful in understanding modern business? Explain.

*2* Why do you think that jargon is so common in business and other technical fields?

# doing **business 1** *e-mail*

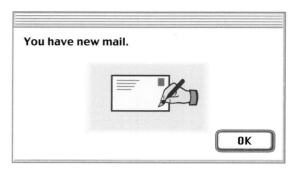

**You have new mail.**

OK

**E-MAIL IMPRESSIONS**

Imagine that you're part of an Internet discussion group for learners of business English around the world. One day the e-mail below arrives from a new member of the group.

Read the e-mail and then talk about these questions.

*1* Which one of these adjectives do you think describes the writer of the e-mail?

**helpful** confident **friendly** intelligent arrogant

*2* What is wrong with the tone of this e-mail? Underline any words or phrases which seem inappropriate.

*3* What is wrong with the content of the e-mail?

*4* Would you reply to this e-mail? If so, what would you say?

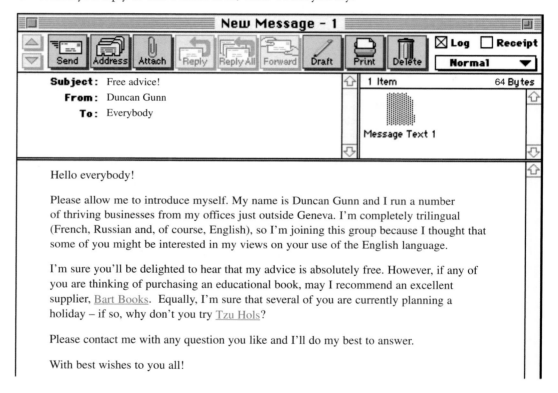

Hello everybody!

Please allow me to introduce myself. My name is Duncan Gunn and I run a number of thriving businesses from my offices just outside Geneva. I'm completely trilingual (French, Russian and, of course, English), so I'm joining this group because I thought that some of you might be interested in my views on your use of the English language.

I'm sure you'll be delighted to hear that my advice is absolutely free. However, if any of you are thinking of purchasing an educational book, may I recommend an excellent supplier, Bart Books.  Equally, I'm sure that several of you are currently planning a holiday – if so, why don't you try Tzu Hols?

Please contact me with any question you like and I'll do my best to answer.

With best wishes to you all!

**INTRODUCING YOURSELF**

**1** Imagine that you want to join an e-mail discussion group about learning business English. Write a short e-mail (on a piece of paper) that introduces yourself and explains what you do and why you want to join the discussion group.

**2** Exchange 'e-mails' with a partner. Read your partner's e-mail and talk about these questions.

*1* Whose style do you think is more suitable for e-mail – yours or your partner's?

*2* When you read the e-mail, did you want to find out more about that person? How could they make themselves sound more interesting?

**KATHRYN AND MIKE**   This is an extract from the novel *The Business* by Iain Banks. It's an e-mail conversation between a senior executive called Kathryn Telman and one of the people who reports to her, Mike Daniels. Daniels is in Tokyo to sign a contract with a man called Kirita Shinizagi.

**1** 👥 Read the e-mails and then answer the questions below.

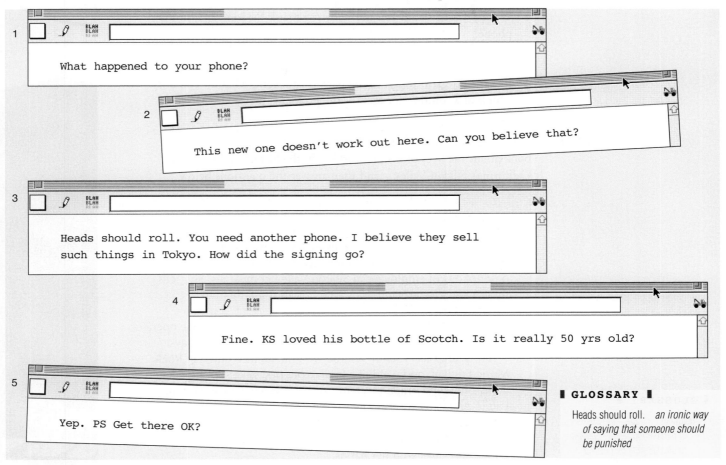

1   What happened to your phone?

2   This new one doesn't work out here. Can you believe that?

3   Heads should roll. You need another phone. I believe they sell such things in Tokyo. How did the signing go?

4   Fine. KS loved his bottle of Scotch. Is it really 50 yrs old?

5   Yep. PS Get there OK?

**▌ GLOSSARY ▌**

Heads should roll.   *an ironic way of saying that someone should be punished*

*1*   Which e-mails are from Kathryn and which are from Mike?
*2*   What's Mike's problem?
*3*   Has Mike succeeded in getting the contract signed?
*4*   What present did Mike give to Mr Shinizagi?

**2** 👥 Is this the kind of e-mail that you would expect work colleagues to send to each other? Why – or why not?

**E-MAIL CONVERSATIONS**

**1** 👥 Have an 'e-mail conversation' by writing on a piece of paper which you pass back and forth between you. Each message should have no more than two sentences in it. Choose one of these subjects.

▌ a programme you saw on TV last night
▌ the price of mobile phones
▌ what you're planning to do at the weekend
▌ what happened to you on your way to work or to the class

**2** 👥 When you've exchanged at least five messages each, one person in each pair should continue the conversation with a partner from another pair.

# doing **business** **2**  *Telephoning*

**GETTING THROUGH**  👥 Talk about these questions.

*1* What phrases would you normally use to ask for someone on the phone?

*2* What problems do you have in getting through to the person you want? Make a list.

*3* If you can't get through to the person you want, what do you do? Think of a solution for each of the problems that you listed in 2.

**A RUSER**  👥 Read this extract from Po Branson's *Nudist on the Late Shift* – a book about the lives of people working in the hi-tech industries of California's Silicon Valley – and then answer the questions below.

> **CLAUDIA** is what is known in the headhunting trade as a 'ruser', meaning one who performs ruses, one who uses surreptitious methods to trick receptionists into giving out names and job descriptions of employees at Silicon Valley companies. She sells these names to research firms which in turn sell them to headhunters.
>
> Claudia works her cellular phone. She dials the Netscape operator, asks for the Website division. When she's connected, she says,
>
> 'Hi, yeah, this is Sarah Velarde with the Lilith/Women in Rock Music Festival, and we'd like to give out free tickets to the concert at the Shoreline Amphitheater next week to any female programmers. Laurie Anderson wants to take a moment to recognize them, have the crowd cheer, that sort of thing.'
>
> Claudia listens for a second. Even when communicating by phone, she talks with her hands.
>
> 'Well, I'm supposed to send them the tickets directly ... Uh-huh ...' She arranges to phone the next day to get the names of those who want to attend.

**GLOSSARY**

**headhunting trade**  *the business of persuading talented people to change jobs by offering them better pay and conditions*

**surreptitious**  *secret and dishonest*

*1* How does a 'ruser' make a living?

*2* Why do you think that the names of employees are so valuable in Silicon Valley?

*3* In your own words, describe Claudia's 'ruse'. Would you be deceived by it?

*Avant garde performance artiste Laurie Anderson is popular with many hi-tech workers.*

**RUSING AND ETHICS**

**1** Which of these statements is closest to your opinion of rusing? Explain your choice.

▮ The logic of the free market encourages rusing, so there's nothing wrong with it.
▮ Rusing should be illegal.
▮ Nobody suffers as a result of rusing, so it's fair enough.
▮ Rusing is based on deception, so it's morally wrong.

**2** Can you think of any situations in which you might use a ruse like Claudia's?

**TWO RUSES**

**1** Quickly read the continuation of the extract. Then listen to the two phone calls. Match each call to one of the ruses described.

> Other common ruses: posing as a reporter; posing as a conference organizer wishing to send literature to product managers; and pretending she's a Pac Bell technician stuck up on a telephone pole outside the building, who needs to verify extensions. One of her favorites is calling a company operator and saying, 'Last night I was playing tennis and got in a doubles game with a programmer from Netscape. I gave him a ride home, but he left his tennis racquet in my car. Now I can't remember his name. Dave or Don or something.'

**2** Choose three adjectives from this list to describe each of the receptionists in the phone calls.

*suspicious*   *cynical*
*polite*   **cautious**   sympathetic
efficient   *helpful*   **curt**

**3** If you were choosing a receptionist, which two of the qualities above would be most important to you?

**RUSING ROLES**

Play the following roles. In each case the receptionist should be as helpful and polite as possible.

▮ Take turns to be ruser and receptionist in the situations that are mentioned in the second part of the extract, but are *not* on the recording.
▮ Again, take turns as ruser and receptionist, but this time the ruser should think of their own ruse to get through to the person that they want to speak to.

# issues

## *Creating an impression*

**THE COMPANY MAN**

This is the novelist Paul Auster's description of his first experience of business life. As a young man, Auster invented a game and arranged a meeting with a businessman from a large toy company to try to sell him the idea.

Read the text and then talk about the questions below.

## The shortest meeting

My talk with the company president turned out to be one of the shortest meetings in the annals of American business. It didn't bother me that the man rejected my game (I was prepared for that, was fully expecting bad news), but he did it in such a chilling way, with so little regard for human decency, that it still causes me pain to think about it. He wasn't much older than I was, this corporate executive, and with his sleek, superbly tailored suit, his blue eyes and blond hair and hard, expressionless face, he looked and acted like the leader of a spy ring. He barely shook my hand, barely said hello, barely acknowledged that I was in the room. No small talk, no pleasantries, no questions. 'Let's see what you have,' he said curtly, and so I reached into my briefcase ...

Hand to Mouth *by Paul Auster*

**▌ GLOSSARY ▌**

annals   *records*

sleek   *smooth and shiny*

tailored   *made*

spy ring   *secret organisation of people involved in espionage*

pleasantries   *polite things to say*

*Paul Auster*

*Company man*

1  What impression does the company executive try to create?
2  Do you think that this is a good image for this kind of person? Explain why – or why not?
3  How would you feel in Paul Auster's position?
4  Has anything similar happened to you or to anyone you know? Tell the story.

**THE CON MAN**

A 'con man' is a person who tricks or swindles other people out of their money, by winning their confidence or trust. Probably the most successful con man of the twentieth century was the European aristocrat, Count Victor Lustig. In the 1920s, he used his skills to 'sell' the Eiffel Tower as scrap metal for a huge sum of money, not once, but twice! He also once tricked the notorious American gangster Al Capone into giving him a large loan – and lived to tell the tale! In the book *The 48 Laws of Power*, Robert Greene describes his image.

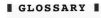 Read about Count Victor Lustig and talk about the questions below.

# *The mysterious count*

COUNT VICTOR LUSTIG was always doing things that were different or seemed to make no sense. He arrived at the best hotels in a limo driven by a Japanese chauffeur; no one had ever seen a Japanese chauffeur before, so this seemed exotic and strange. He dressed in the most expensive clothing, but always with something – a medal, a flower, an armband – out of place. He received telegrams at all hours, brought to him by his Japanese chauffeur – and he would tear them up with utter nonchalance. (In fact, they were fakes, completely blank.) In the evenings, he sat alone in the dining room, reading a large and impressive book, smiling at people, yet remaining aloof. Within a few days, the entire hotel would be fascinated by this strange man.

**■ GLOSSARY ■**

limo   *large luxurious car*
nonchalance   *calmness and a lack of anxiety*
aloof   *distant, without interest in one's surroundings*

1   Would people in the modern world trust a person with Count Lustig's image? Why – or why not?
2   In the modern business world, what kind of person would the perfect con man or con woman be? Think about the way he or she would travel, the clothes they would wear, the places they would go to and the way they would behave.
3   What kind of modern businessperson wouldn't you trust? Describe their image.

**IMPRESSIONS AND YOU**

 Discuss these questions.

1   How often do you think your first impressions of people are right? Think of one example when they've been correct and one time when they've been wrong.
2   Do you think that the first impression people have of you is the right impression? Think of one way in which you think you are often misunderstood and ask others in the group for their advice.

# 2 managing change

**THE FACTS OF CHANGE**  Read these facts about the way in which the world is changing and talk about the questions which follow.

> Before the invention of the electric light in the 1880s, people slept for an average of 10 hours a night. In 1997, a typical employee of a multinational company slept for an average of just 6.5 hours a night.

1 Do you think that this is a positive or negative change in people's lifestyles?
2 Can you think of two other major changes in people's lifestyles that have happened over the past 100 years?

> In 1960 in the USA, there were around 5,000 people over the age of 100. By 2010, there will be over 5,000,000.

What problems and opportunities does this change present for business?

> In the USA, it took around 50 years for radio to win an audience of 50 million people. The Internet had 50 million users within just 4 years of its introduction.

1 Do you think that the Internet is spreading as quickly around the rest of the world?
2 What practical differences has it made to your life?

> Moore's law says that the price of computing power halves every 2 years. If the car industry had developed at this speed over the past 30 years, you would be able to buy a new BMW today for just $2.

1 Are there any signs that the revolution in computers is coming to a halt?
2 Would it really be a good thing if a new BMW cost just $2? Explain your thinking.

**A STORY OF CHANGE**    **1**    Read this story and in your own words explain why the twelve monkeys at the end behaved as they did.

**I**N AN EXPERIMENT, scientists put twelve monkeys in a room which was empty except for a tall pole with a bunch of bananas at the top. Just above the bananas, hidden in the ceiling, there was a shower head.

It didn't take long for one of the older monkeys to spot the bananas and it greedily climbed up the pole to grab them. But when it got near the top, the scientists sprayed it with freezing water and the monkey screamed and jumped back down. A few minutes later, another monkey tried to reach the bananas, with exactly the same result.

Shortly after this, the scientists made two changes. They took one of the monkeys out of the room and replaced it with another one. They also disconnected the shower head.

After some time, the new monkey started to climb the pole to get the bananas. But before it could get too high, the other monkeys pulled it back, screaming and pointing to the ceiling.

Over the next few hours, the scientists replaced all the other monkeys in the room, one by one, until all twelve of the original monkeys were gone. And, although none of the monkeys that were now in the room had ever seen the shower working, not one of them climbed the pole to eat the delicious bananas at the top.

**❚ GLOSSARY ❚**

shower head    *the part of the shower which water comes out of*

**2**    Now discuss these questions.

*1*  Have you ever been in a situation where humans behaved in a similar way? Describe it.
*2*  In business life, can you think of any parallels for the moment in the story when the scientists disconnected the shower head?
*3*  In what ways could this story be a lesson for business? Give examples.

**CHANGE AND YOU**    **1**    What do you think are the three biggest changes in business in the past five years? How have you reacted to them?

**2**    Despite all the talk of change, at the end of 1999 ...
... only 50% of the world's population had ever used a telephone ...
... only 20% of the world's population had ever flown in a plane ...
... and only a tiny, tiny minority had ever surfed the Internet.

Do you think we overestimate the importance of change in the modern business world?

# GRAMMAR REVIEW

**JACK WELCH'S CAREER**

Jack Welch retired from his job as CEO of General Electric in 2000. Read this article from *The Economist*, which talks about some of his achievements in his time as the company's boss.

1 Make a list of Jack Welch's achievements.
2 Notice that the article was written in 1999 (before Jack Welch retired), so all his achievements are described in the present perfect. If you were writing the article today (after his retirement), what changes would you need to make to the verbs?

## JACK WELCH the businessman's favourite businessman

At General Electric, Mr Welch has established a culture of constant self-transformation. His career has been built not on new technology, but on products such as turbines and lightbulbs. Thanks to his continual revolution after becoming boss in 1981, GE's revenues have quadrupled and its share price has risen thirtyfold.

There are reasons to be sceptical about Mr Welch. In an age of small companies, he runs not just a big firm but a conglomerate. But much of GE's growth has come from skills such as passing ideas around and the embrace of globalisation, services and the Internet. Mr Welch hasn't proved that big companies are better than smaller ones. What he has shown is that speed and adaptability count more than size.

*The Economist 18.9.99*

### ■ CHECK

The **past simple** is used to refer to finished actions which happened at a definite time in the past.

*He worked for General Electric for ten years, but he retired last month.*

But when referring to a period of time from the past up to the present, use the **present perfect**.

*He has been with General Electric for six years (and he hasn't retired yet.)*

■ *For more on the past simple and present perfect, turn to page 139.* ■

**PRESENT PERFECT OR PAST SIMPLE?**

Check that you remember when to use the past simple and present perfect by putting the verbs in brackets into the correct tense.

1 She (never be) _____ to Kyoto, but she (go) _____ to Tokyo last year.
2 Our shareholders (receive) _____ our annual report last week, but I'm sure most of them (not read) _____ it yet.
3 I (have) _____ this car for five years and I (never have) _____ an accident.
4 I (speak) _____ to Mario yesterday afternoon, but I (not see) _____ him since then.
5 They (cancel) _____ the meeting yesterday and they (do) _____ the same thing again today.
6 Our air-conditioning system (break down) _____ last week, so we (install) _____ a new one.
7 Yves (be) _____ here this morning, but he (just leave) _____ the office.
8 She (have to) _____ work late last night and she (not go) _____ to bed until three o'clock this morning.
9 He (not play) _____ tennis since he (break) _____ his arm.
10 We (book) _____ the flights last month, but we (not book) _____ the hotel yet.

# *Present perfect (simple and continuous)*

**COMPLAINING ABOUT CHANGE**

**1** 🎧 Listen to the recording of two office workers complaining and answer these questions.

*1* What change in their work conditions are they particularly angry about?
*2* Who is responsible for this change?

**2** 🎧 Listen again and note down two or three answers to both these questions.

*1* What hasn't their boss done?
*2* What has she been doing?

**3** 👥 Notice that two tenses are used in the questions and answers above. Can you explain why?

---

### ▌ CHECK

The present perfect simple and continuous talk about something that started in the past and is still continuing or has only recently finished. Often, either tense can be used.

*I've worked for this company since 1996.*
*I've been working here since 1996.*

The **present perfect continuous** emphasises the continuity of an action; it also often describes activities which have been happening over a period of time.

*She's been talking on the phone for hours.*

The **present perfect simple** is more often used to describe situations in which little or nothing has happened, or to describe activities which have been completed.

*He hasn't come in since Tuesday.*
*They've had three meetings this week.*

▌ *For more on this, turn to page 142.* ▌

---

**SIMPLE OR CONTINUOUS?**

Check that you remember when to use the present perfect simple and present perfect continuous by putting the verbs in brackets into the correct tense.

*1* He (work) _____ on the report all week.
*2* I (not smoke) _____ a cigarette so far this week.
*3* She looks impatient. How long (she wait) _____?
*4* He (play) _____ football since he (be) _____ twelve.
*5* She (talk) _____ to her client on the phone for the last twenty minutes.
*6* I (expect) _____ this letter for ages.
*7* The office (not be cleaned) _____ for over a week.
*8* They (take) _____ their holiday at the same place for years.
*9* The network (be) _____ down all morning.
*10* He seems very nervous behind the wheel. How long (he drive) _____?

**THE PAST AND YOU**

👥 Think of five questions to ask your partner in an imaginary job interview situation. Use the past simple, present perfect and present perfect continuous.

## *Business changes*

**vocabulary**

**BUZZWORDS**

**1** 👥 Here are five words that are often used to describe the way in which business life is changing. Match them to the definitions.

> *outsourcing*  *hotdesking*  *telecommuting*
> *downsizing*  **globalisation**

- ▮ the tendency for the world economy to work as one unit
- ▮ people working from home
- ▮ reducing the number of people in a company
- ▮ people sharing their work space with others
- ▮ buying services from other companies rather than doing them in-house

**2** 👥👥 Which of the above are changes for the better and which are changes for the worse? Explain your views.

**THE US MANAGER**

👥👥 Read the text below from *The Economist* and answer these questions.

*1* What two words is 'affluenza' made up of, and what does it mean?
*2* Why do modern managers work longer hours than in the past?
*3* Why are managers less powerful than they used to be?
*4* Why are they feeling more insecure?
*5* Which three of the buzzwords above are mentioned? Which buzzword isn't mentioned but is referred to?

# Overworked and overpaid: the American manager

**M**anagers are miserable and this does their companies no good. Consultants talk about companies producing burnt-out 'human cinders' and the rich-but-unhappy syndrome known as 'affluenza'. Why? There are four main reasons:

1 Most companies have thinned the layers of corporate bureaucracy, so most managers work longer hours. An investment bank will these days ask three managers to do the work that five did in the past, and pay them more. At the same time, thanks to globalisation, many managers spend a large amount of time travelling, with many hours in jumbo jets.

2 Managers have been forced to give some of their power away to teams. Firms have also outsourced operations that were once in their managers' control. Status-enhancing perks, such as executive dining rooms, disappeared long ago; now some companies expect their managers to be out on the road so often that they are forced to 'hotdesk' and share offices.

3 Thanks to flatter management structures, the old reliable ladder of career advancement has gone. Careers tend to proceed in great jumps. Those who are left out feel they are going nowhere.

4 Above all, there is the danger of losing your job. In 1998, American firms sacked 677,795 people. Many of the extra profits of the 1990s have come from thinning managerial ranks. Even at the top, job security is not what it used to be.

*The Economist 30.1.99*

**OLD AND NEW COMPANIES**

**1**  Here are some terms from the article. Which of these terms do you associate with old companies and which are associated with new companies?

*career ladder* **corporate bureaucracy**

flat management structures

*job security*     team working

**2** What ideas about old and new companies can you add to the ones above?

**MANAGERIAL BENEFITS**

Talk about these questions.

*1* The article says that many benefits that increase a manager's status ('status-enhancing perks') have disappeared. Here are some other benefits that managers have enjoyed in the past. How many of these do you think are also disappearing?

▌a company car          ▌business class travel
▌a personal assistant    ▌a large comfortable office

*2* What new benefits have managers been offered in the past few years?

**BUSINESS CHANGES AND YOU**

Discuss these points.

*1* How many of the problems mentioned in the article also affect managers in your country?
*2* What problems faced by modern managers could you add to *The Economist*'s list?
*3* Would you rather be poor and happy, or would you prefer to suffer from 'affluenza'?

# doing business 1 *Breaking bad news*

**EUPHEMISMS**   A euphemism is a less direct way of saying something that is unpleasant. Here are six ways of talking about an unpleasant part of business life.

*downsizing*     **firing**     *sacking*

*letting people go*     *rightsizing*     **restructuring**

Decide what situation these words describe and rank them from the most brutal (1) to the most humane (6).

**MORE BAD NEWS**   **1**  These sentences contain euphemisms for other kinds of bad news. Match the euphemisms on the left with the bad news on the right.

| | |
|---|---|
| I'm afraid we're going to have to move our account. | I can't pay you. |
| I'm sorry to say we've adjusted your remuneration to take account of the changing circumstances. | He's dead. |
| It may come as a shock to learn that he's passed away. | We're going to cut your pay. |
| I have to say I'm a little financially embarrassed at the moment. | I was lying. |
| Unfortunately, I was being economical with the truth. | You've lost the contract. |

**2**  Notice that each of the above sentences begins with a phrase to 'soften the blow' of breaking the bad news, e.g. *I'm afraid ...* . What other phrases do you know that do this?

**BARNEVIK AND ATTITUDE**   Percy Barnevik is one of the most respected managers in the world and has shown that he is prepared to take some tough decisions. Read what he says about downsizing a company and talk about the questions below.

> Whether you call it downsizing or firing people, it's a serious human problem. I detest the macho view of some Americans who rank managers by their toughness. It can be a bloodbath. To downsize effectively, you have to have empathy with the people who are losing their jobs. You have to pay money, take time, handle them with honesty and respect. What you say to them has a lot to do with the attitude of the survivors: whether they see the company as a money machine or keep their respect and trust for it.

*1* How different is Percy Barnevik's attitude to yours?
*2* What are the business reasons for handling the bad news in this way? Do you agree with his ideas on this?

**LEAVING LAS VEGAS**

At the start of the movie *Leaving Las Vegas*, we see that the main character, Ben, is having serious personal problems. He is becoming an alcoholic and has started behaving erratically. He is soon called into his boss's office at the Hollywood film studio where he works and is told that he is being dismissed from his job.

Read the script and then talk about these questions.

*1* What would Percy Barnevik think of the way that the bad news is broken?
*2* How do you think the boss handles breaking the bad news?
*3* What sort of questions would you ask if you found yourself in Ben's position? Think about these possibilities.

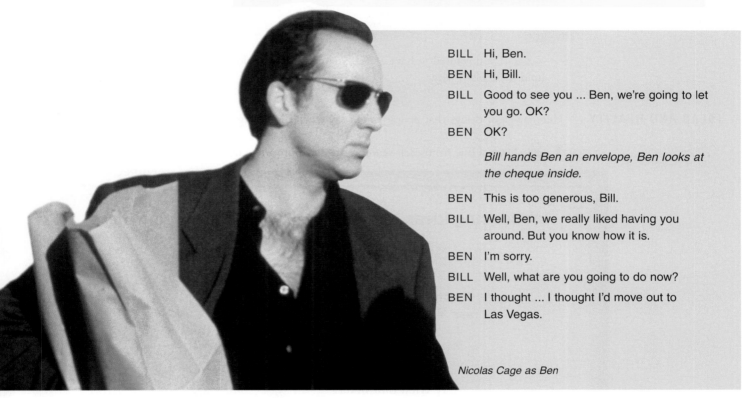

more money?    **a second chance?**    *training?*

BILL   Hi, Ben.

BEN    Hi, Bill.

BILL   Good to see you ... Ben, we're going to let you go. OK?

BEN    OK?

*Bill hands Ben an envelope, Ben looks at the cheque inside.*

BEN    This is too generous, Bill.

BILL   Well, Ben, we really liked having you around. But you know how it is.

BEN    I'm sorry.

BILL   Well, what are you going to do now?

BEN    I thought ... I thought I'd move out to Las Vegas.

*Nicolas Cage as Ben*

**BAD NEWS ROLES**

Role play these situations. In each case, the person who receives the bad news should try to ask questions or find other ways of achieving the best possible outcome for him/herself. (If you like, try giving the bad news in the style of Percy Barnevik or Bill from the Hollywood studio – or both!)

▌**A** You are a new senior manager in a multinational company. You have to tell **B**, a long-serving middle manager, that there is no longer a job for him/her.

▌**B** Your Internet start-up has just lost a large amount of money. You have to break the bad news to **A**, a venture capitalist who has invested heavily in the business.

▌**A** You are the purchasing manager at a large car plant. You have been supplied with electric motors for many years by **B**, who owns a small family business. You have to tell **B** that you are going to terminate their contract and buy in future from a bigger, cheaper supplier.

▌**B** You are a sales manager who has to tell **A**, a salesperson, that they have just missed their sales targets for the year and so won't be getting their usual bonus.

# doing **business** 2 *Discussing ideas*

**AWAYDAYS**

**1** When they are faced with the need to do some creative thinking, some companies send a team of employees away from their offices to work together in a hotel or maybe even a camp in the countryside.

Do you think that getting away from your normal working environment creates the right atmosphere in which to discuss business ideas?

**2** Even if you don't go away somewhere, you don't have to meet in a standard meeting room around a normal table. You can have a meeting in a park, in a nearby bar or cafe, or even just standing up instead of sitting down.

If you wanted to have a creative business discussion with colleagues, where would you hold it? Explain why.

**IDEAS AND REALITY**

Here are eight things that people might say when discussing ideas.

**1** Draw a line from each sentence to the appropriate heading.

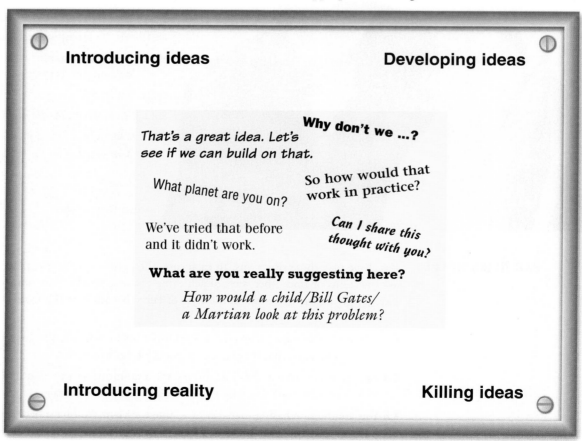

**Introducing ideas**

**Developing ideas**

Why don't we ...?

*That's a great idea. Let's see if we can build on that.*

What planet are you on?

So how would that work in practice?

We've tried that before and it didn't work.

*Can I share this thought with you?*

**What are you really suggesting here?**

*How would a child/Bill Gates/ a Martian look at this problem?*

**Introducing reality**

**Killing ideas**

**2** Think of at least one sentence that you can add under each of the four headings. Compare your sentences with others in the class.

**BRAINSTORMING**    Brainstorming is an attempt by a group of people to generate a number of ideas about a situation or problem.

**1** 👥 Brainstorm ideas to solve these problems and then compare your ideas with others in the class.

> *Dropping litter*
> **A city in the Netherlands has a problem with litter and its streets are full of all kinds of rubbish. At the moment, there is a fine of 25 guilders for anyone who is caught dropping litter on the streets, but it is clearly not a very effective deterrent. Can you think of some ideas to solve the problem?**

> *Bike theft*
> **Police in a university city in England were under pressure to reduce the number of bicycles that were stolen on its streets every year. They knew that they weren't facing a group of organised criminals; in fact, their research showed that the majority of bikes were stolen by students on their way home from the pub late at night. What ideas do you have for reducing the number of stolen bikes?**

**2** To find out what the Dutch city authorities and the British police really did in these situations, turn to page 125.

**THINKING OUTSIDE YOUR BOX**    Problems can sometimes be solved by looking at ordinary things or familiar situations in new ways. It's a technique that's often used by radical artists. For example, in the late 1970s, punk rockers created a new fashion industry by realising that safety pins could become earrings and that rubbish bags could be worn as dresses. Today this technique, called 'thinking outside your box', is used by many management consultants!

👥 Talk about some of these questions, then compare your ideas with the rest of the class. (Be radical!)

▌ When your office (or classroom) is not being used, how could you make money from the space?

▌ CDs are obviously designed to play music, but what else could you do with them?

▌ How many different uses for a paper clip can you think of?

**IDEAS AND YOU**    👥 Talk about these questions.

*1* Think of a recent problem in your working life. Do you think any of the methods on these pages could help you to solve it?

*2* If you were asked to organise a meeting to discuss ideas, how would you structure the discussion?

# issues

*Work space*

**THE OPEN PLAN OFFICE**

 Look at this picture of an office from the 1960 movie *The Apartment*, then talk about these questions.

1  In what ways is this work space different from the place where you work?
2  What are the good and bad points of working in this kind of 'open-plan' office?

**THE DESK**

In her novel about office life, *The Temp*, Serena Mackesey writes about the importance of a desk in the workplace.

 Read this extract and then talk about the questions below.

You learn a lot about people from their desks. In the alien world of the office, the desk is a little extension of home, a place on which you can stamp your identity. People rely on these mementos of their individuality to give them the sense of security essential to handling stress, keeping their tempers, generally getting through the day.

It seems to me that firms who want to stamp their corporate identity on their employees by imposing rules about these things are making a big mistake. I've come across countless clean-desk policies, where nothing unrelated to the job in hand is allowed on a surface and everything has to be tidied away at the end of the day. This has to be the most pernicious of all the experimental work practices of the nineties.

▐ **GLOSSARY** ▐

mementos  *reminders*
pernicious  *bad, wrong*

1  How important is your desk to you? Do you agree that a desk in the office is an extension of home?
2  How would you feel about working in an office with a clean-desk policy?
3  Can you think of any other experimental work practices? How useful do you think they are?
4  Do you think that the traditional desk in the traditional office will change over the next few years? If so, in what ways?

*The new Freemans building*

## FUTONS AND FISH TANKS

Some companies have designed their office buildings in revolutionary new ways. Read this description of a new office building and talk about the questions below.

Here is a novel way of tackling stress: install futons, fish tanks and wishing wells in the office. Freemans, the mail-order company, is spending £20 million building what it describes as 'a perfect working environment', which will incorporate these features.

Futons will be installed in special 'anti-stress' rooms, and there will be fish tanks for stressed-out people to gaze at. Water will be the theme, with partitions that appear to have water cascading down them, and a wishing well which the company has named 'Freemans Fountain of Youth'.

I wonder if Freemans could have created the same beneficial effect on its employees' mental health at rather less cost.

*Sense and Nonsense in the Office by Lucy Kellaway*

**▌ GLOSSARY ▌**

futon   *a low sofa or bed*

to cascade   *to fall*

*1* In what ways are Freemans' offices different from a normal office building?
*2* Do you think that you'd like to work in a building like this? Why – or why not?
*3* Do you think the money Freemans is investing in its employees' mental health is money well spent?
*4* What is the most unusual feature that you have seen or heard about in a workplace? What was the purpose of it?

## TELEWORKING

Around fifty million Americans do at least some of their work from home and the number of people teleworking is rising every year. In their book, *The Witch Doctors*, John Micklethwait and Adrian Wooldridge write about its growing popularity.

Read the text and then discuss the questions below.

> The best argument for the efficiency of staying at home is usually the inefficiency of going to work. One study of 90,000 managers by Booz Allen and Hamilton found that people waste a quarter of their time at work. Add up the hours spent in pointless meetings, commuting and hanging around the coffee machine and you should find this is an underestimate.

*1* How much time do you estimate that people waste in your workplace (or a workplace that you know)? What do they spend this time doing?
*2* Do you think that people waste more or less time if they work at home?
*3* What are the main disadvantages of working from home?

## WORK SPACE AND YOU

If you could design your company's offices, what would you do? Work together to draw a simple plan and explain the advantages of your ideas to the rest of the class.

# 3  the **boss**

**LEADERSHIP OR MANAGEMENT?**

Companies have to be led, not managed. It's not that difficult to manage companies. What they've got to be is led.

*Greg Dyke, Director General of the UK's state broadcaster, the BBC*

 What do you think are the differences between leadership and management?

**THE BOSSES SAY ...** Here are five things that well-known people have said about leadership and management. Discuss which of the quotations are about management and which are about leadership, and choose some of these words to complete the sentences.

*lead* *leadership* management
leading **managing**
leader *manager* *manage*

A _____'s job should be based on a task to be performed in order to attain the company's objectives.

*Peter Drucker, business guru*

A _____ is someone who knows what they want to achieve and can communicate that.

*Margaret Thatcher, former British Prime Minister*

To _____ is to forecast and plan, to organise, to command, to co-ordinate and to control.

*Henri Fayol, French writer and industrialist*

The task of the _____ is to get his people from where they are to where they have not been.

*Henry Kissinger, American diplomat*

_____ is like holding a dove in your hand. Squeeze too tight, you kill it. Open your hand too much, you let it go.

*Tommy Lasorda, coach of the L.A. Dodgers baseball team*

**LEADERS AND CONDUCTORS**

In their book *Leaders*, Warren Bennis and Burt Nanus compare the work of a business leader with the job of the conductor of an orchestra.

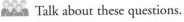 Read the text and then compare the work of a business and an orchestra by answering these questions.

1 According to Bennis and Nanus, who does the real work in a business and in an orchestra?
2 What does getting the 'right work done at the right time' mean in both cases?
3 What does 'desired impact on the outside world' mean for both of them?
4 Can you think of any other parallels between the work of a conductor and the work of a business leader?
5 What other jobs outside the business world have parallels with the work of a business leader?

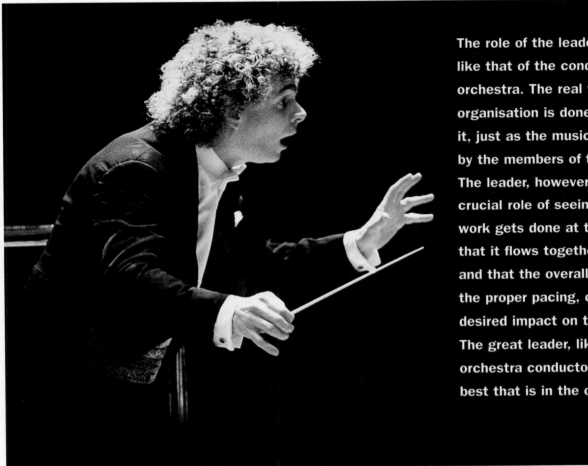

The role of the leader is much like that of the conductor of an orchestra. The real work of the organisation is done by the people in it, just as the music is produced only by the members of the orchestra. The leader, however, serves the crucial role of seeing that the right work gets done at the right time, that it flows together harmoniously and that the overall performance has the proper pacing, co-ordination and desired impact on the outside world. The great leader, like the great orchestra conductor, calls forth the best that is in the organisation.

**BOSSES AND YOU**

Talk about these questions.

1 Which of these people do you think are more like managers and which are more like leaders?
  ▮ the president or prime minister of your country
  ▮ the boss of an organisation
  ▮ a teacher or trainer
2 What qualities do these people share with the conductor of an orchestra?
3 Who are the best and the worst bosses that you've had? Give reasons.

# GRAMMAR REVIEW

**ATTILA THE HUN**   Attila the Hun was a leader of the barbarian tribes who fought against the Roman Empire in the first half of the fifth century. He has been famous throughout history for his savagery and cruelty. But, a few years ago, he was famous as the subject of a bestselling business book. Read this extract, in which Attila is talking about some of his management secrets.

What modern business words would you use to replace these words?

*chieftain*   subordinate leader   *tribes*

Our leaders – you chieftains and valued warriors gathered here tonight – must learn the responsibilities of office.

- Chieftains and leaders are responsible for establishing the atmosphere in which they lead. This atmosphere *may* have periods of change, even as the seasons change. Nonetheless, our leaders can and must control the spirit of our tribes.

- Chieftains and subordinate leaders must learn the responsibilities of their office. Without such knowledge, how *can* they fulfil their duties?

- Chieftains *should* not misuse their power. Such action causes great friction and leads to rebellion in the tribe or nation.

- Chieftains *must* understand that the spirit of the law is greater than its letter.

The things I have told you tonight are the secrets to leadership success at any level of office. They may seem to you to be common knowledge. Alas, they may be, but they are not so common in practice.

▌ **GLOSSARY** ▌

alas   *unfortunately*

Leadership Secrets of Attila the Hun *by Wess Roberts*

**MODALS REVIEW**   **1**  Look at the four sentences in the text which contain modal verbs in italic. Which of these sentences ...

- ▌ talks about a logical possibility?
- ▌ talks about an obligation?
- ▌ talks about something which is generally possible?
- ▌ gives advice?

**2**  Which three of the modal verbs in italics can be replaced by one of the verbs in the box, without changing the meaning of the sentence?

*might*  have to  ᵒᵘᵍʰᵗ to

**3**  Find some more modal verbs in the text. Can you replace them with other modals without changing the meaning of the sentences?

▌ *For more on modals and related verbs, see pages 135 and 136.* ▌

# Modals and related verbs

**PRESENT LEADERS**

1 Complete these sentences, using modals and related verbs from the text opposite in either the positive or the negative form. In some cases, there may be more than one correct answer.

1 Leaders _____ publicise their mistakes. If they do, they _____ expect the respect of the public.

2 Although they _____ be very powerful, business leaders _____ break the laws of the country in which they're based.

3 Leaders _____ do everything themselves. They _____ set clear targets and learn to delegate.

4 In the short term, technology _____ change the way we work, but a leader _____ have a long term view.

5 Good leaders _____ listen to the opinions of their subordinates, but ultimately they _____ take their own decisions.

2 Compare your answers. If you have chosen different modals, is there also a difference in meaning?

**PAST LEADERS**

Fill the gaps in these sentences about leaders of the past, using appropriate modals and related verbs in the past. Use either the positive or negative form.

1 In the past, military leaders _____ obey the orders of their king or queen.

2 In the last century, the leaders of industry _____ dismiss workers whenever they liked.

3 Until recently, political leaders _____ worry too much about the media's opinion of them.

4 Business leaders of the early twentieth century _____ get information about foreign markets very easily.

5 Leaders of the past _____ work under great pressure, but at least they _____ answer e-mails and phone calls.

**ATTILA AND YOU**

Look again at the text opposite and talk about the following.

1 How would you explain Attila's advice to a modern businessperson?

2 Can you think of any modern examples to support Attila's advice?

3 Think of three pieces of advice for the modern business leader that you would add to Attila's list.

## Describing people

**VOCABULARY**

**AN EVENING WITH DR O'REILLY**

In his book, *Company Man*, the writer Anthony Sampson describes a party at the home of the former Chief Executive Officer of Heinz, Dr Tony O'Reilly.

**1** Read the text and then answer these questions.

*1* Scott Fitzgerald wrote about glamorous social events in America in the 1920s. In what ways do you think the party is similar?
*2* What's the connection between mushroom-farming and management?
*3* Why does Anthony Sampson think the party is typical of Irish Catholic culture?
*4* Why might a modern management guru approve of the party?

**2** What do you think Tony O'Reilly's objectives were in holding this party?

**POSITION**

Here are five words from the text which are used to talk about Dr O'Reilly's position. Look at them and then answer the questions below.

chairman    executive    entrepreneur    tycoon    chief executive

**1** Which word means ...

*1* ... the head of the board of directors of a company?
*2* ... a kind of businessman who starts businesses and takes risks?
*3* ... a person in an organisation who takes decisions?
*4* ... a very wealthy and successful businessperson?
*5* ... the person with the top job in a company who makes its most important decisions?

**2** Think of another businessperson that each of the words in the box could describe. (Each person could be from your company or from the business world in general.)

**CHARACTER**

**1** These adjectives are often used to describe a person's social presence. Choose one adjective from each of these pairs which best describes Dr O'Reilly. In each case find a sentence or phrase in the text to justify your choice. (You may need to use a dictionary to help you.) Compare your ideas with others in the class.

| | |
|---|---|
| charming | ingratiating |
| charismatic | attractive |
| aggressive | dominating |
| aloof | gregarious |
| vivacious | dynamic |

**2** Which of the adjectives could describe your boss (or another boss that you know)? Think of other suitable adjectives to describe this person that you could add to the list.

**THE COMPANY MAN**

Anthony Sampson says that the Heinz people saw Dr O'Reilly as 'the personification of the company' – the person who represented all its values.

**1** If O'Reilly was the personification of Heinz, what kind of company do you think it was?

**2** Think of another businessperson who is the 'personification' of their company. In what ways are they different from Heinz and Dr O'Reilly?

# An evening with Dr O'Reilly

In the summer of 1994, several coach-loads of company men and their wives arrived at the grey Georgian mansion of Castlemartin outside Dublin, on the banks of the Liffey. They were shown into a hall filled with modern Irish paintings round a handsome double staircase, where a butler offered them drinks and showed them into a marquee. At the centre of the marquee a tall, commanding Irishman welcomed each of them with a joke and an intimate smile before they mingled and sat down at dining tables round the dance floor.

It could have been a scene from Scott Fitzgerald. In fact it was the annual outing for senior Heinz executives who had flown in from Pittsburgh and elsewhere. The host was Dr Tony O'Reilly, the chairman and chief executive who was also Ireland's leading entrepreneur with his own interests around the world. O'Reilly had become the most legendary of the new master-tribe of industrial entrepreneurs: in America he had been billed as the highest-paid executive, earning $105 million in 1991 and 1992, apart from his own free-booting deals which made him the richest man in Ireland. Like all tycoons, O'Reilly created his own aura.

Down at the dinner table in the marquee he was making everyone feel taller while dominating their talk. My neighbour, a minister in the Dublin government, was telling a joke about an Irishman discussing styles of management with an American and a Japanese: 'We follow the mushroom principle,' says the Irishman. 'Keep them in the dark and cover them with muck.' O'Reilly asked him what we were talking about. He replied, 'Management,' and O'Reilly told him: 'Talk to him about South Africa.'

The marquee embraced two almost opposite cultures: the Protestant ethic of the Pittsburgh company men, dedicated to their specialised tasks, and the Catholic ethic of the Irish, putting everything in the context of family, big heart and universal values. But the puritanism was rapidly dissolving in a sea of jokes and alcohol as O'Reilly and his wife Chryss were transforming the business outing into a family party. And the Irish, whatever their past business shortcomings, were showing all the talents which management gurus were now stressing: communicating casually, escaping from hierarchies, inspiring enthusiasm, relating work to the family. The party ended at 3.30 am, with O'Reilly showing no signs of sagging, when the coaches drove the Heinz people back to their Dublin hotels.

The next morning, they emerged bleary-eyed. 'You're lucky ever to get to bed before 3 am,' explained one Pittsburgh man who had often stayed at Castlemartin. O'Reilly always noticed who left early, said another, and recorded that they lacked stamina. Every Heinz man seemed to see himself in the context of the boss, watching him, speculating about him and regarding him as the personification of the company.

## ▌ GLOSSARY ▌

| | |
|---|---|
| marquee *a large tent used for social events* | muck *dirt (or worse!)* |
| to mingle *to mix socially* | to sag *to run out of energy* |
| free-booting *independent* | bleary-eyed *with sleepy,* |
| aura *a feeling that seems to surround a person* | *unfocused eyes* |

# doing **business 1** *Delegating*

**WHEN TO DELEGATE?**
All successful leaders and managers have to learn to delegate – in other words, they have to get other people to do some part of their work.

**1** In which of these situations do you think that you should delegate work?
- when you don't want to do something
- when you're too busy to do something
- when the task is time-consuming and boring
- when the task is interesting and motivating

**2** Think of other situations when you would delegate.

**IN THE COMPANY OF MEN**
*In the Company of Men* is a film set in a big American corporation. In this scene Chad (Aaron Eckhart) is being asked to do something by his boss, Howard (Matt Malloy).

Read the script and answer these questions.
*1* What does Howard want Chad to do?
*2* Why has he decided to delegate this task?
*3* Why doesn't Chad want to do it?
*4* Which of these adjectives describes Howard's style of delegation?

*tentative*
*dictatorial*
assertive

| | |
|---|---|
| HOWARD | So, how are things going? |
| CHAD | OK. Busy ... |
| HOWARD | Yeah? |
| CHAD | Oh yeah ... Customers, you know. But hitting my deadlines, so ... |
| HOWARD | Hey, appreciate that. Love to have this whole thing in place by the holiday ... you know, I know this is last minute, but ... I was thinking maybe you'd fly back over the break and deliver that stuff, make the presentation. If it's all right ... they wanna know what we've been doing, so it's umm ... yeah. |
| CHAD | I thought you were set to go back on that. |
| HOWARD | Well, I was, but you know, I just got so much stuff piling up down there ... |
| CHAD | Like what, it's the weekend ... |
| HOWARD | Well, you know, things ... |
| CHAD | Well, why don't we send this John guy? He's up to speed on it. |
| HOWARD | I was gonna, but he doesn't know the city or the players back there. I think you'd just go a long way towards selling the changes we implemented in the package ... if you're OK with that. If you're not ... |

| | |
|---|---|
| CHAD | Sure. I'm salary. There's no such thing as holidays ... Leave it on your desk, I'll pick it up on Friday. |
| HOWARD | Terrific. I'll keep an eye on things at this end and we can meet on Monday, review it all ... Appreciate it, Chad. |

**▍ GLOSSARY ▍**

hitting my deadlines  *finishing my tasks on time*

He's up to speed on it.  *He knows everything about it.*

players  *people involved*

I'm salary.  *I'm an employee.*

**INCOMPLETE SENTENCES**   In the film script, the characters often don't finish their sentences. Look again at these sentences and think about what they would have said if they'd finished them.

| | |
|---|---|
| But hitting my deadlines, so ... | *there's no need for you to worry about anything.* |
| They wanna know what we've been doing, so it's ... | |
| Like what, it's the weekend ... | |
| Well, you know, things ... | |
| If you're OK with that. If you're not ... | |

**DELEGATING STYLES**

**1** When delegating to Chad, Howard follows the three main steps on the left. Match them to the three phrases on the right that he uses.

*1* He asks Chad to do the job.
*2* He explains why he wants him to do it.
*3* He persuades him to do it.

*a* I just got so much stuff piling up down there ...
*b* I know this is last minute, but I was thinking maybe you'd fly back over the break ...
*c* I think you'd just go a long way towards selling the changes we implemented in the package ...

**2**   Listen to a woman delegating work to a colleague and make a note of the three phrases that she uses for each of the three steps above.

> *1 I know this is late in the day, but I wonder if ...*

**3**   How would you describe the woman's style of delegation? Do you think it's more or less effective than Howard's style?

**IN HOWARD'S SHOES**   If you were in Howard's position, what other things could you say to Chad? Talk about these questions.

*1* What other phrases do you know to ask someone else to do something?
*2* What other explanations could you give for wanting to delegate the job?
*3* What else could you say to persuade Chad to fly out and make the presentation?

**DELEGATING ROLES**   Role play these situations.

**▌A** You are supposed to attend a conference abroad next weekend, but you have been invited to a friend's party on the same day. Try to persuade **B**, a colleague, to go to the conference instead of you.

**B** You are a colleague of **A** and you're free the weekend of the conference, but you've been working very hard for the past few weeks and would like to have a weekend's rest.

**▌B** You are **A**'s boss and you are supposed to chair a meeting tomorrow, but you have too much other work to do. Ask **A** if s/he will take your place.

**A** Although replacing your boss at the meeting could be a good move for your career, this is the third time this month that **B** has asked you to do this and you're getting worried about your own deadlines.

# doing **business** 2 *Motivating*

**SPEECHES**  At the start of the movie *Glengarry Glen Ross*, a sales director tries to motivate his team of real-estate salesmen by giving them a motivational speech.

Read this extract from his speech and talk about these questions.

1 How would you feel if your boss spoke to you in this way?
2 Which do you think would motivate you more – the chance of winning a car or the fear of losing your job?
3 What other factors do you think motivate people to work hard?
4 If you wanted to motivate a team of salespeople, what would you say to them?

> The good news is – you're fired. The bad news is you've got – all you've got – is one week to get your jobs back. Have I got your attention now? Good. Because we're adding a little something to this month's sales competition. First prize, as you know, is a Cadillac Eldorado. Second prize is a set of steak knives. Third prize is 'You're fired'. Do you get the picture? Are you laughing now?

*Boss Alec Baldwin in* Glengarry Glen Ross

**SONGS**  Many companies use songs to motivate their employees. Here is part of a Microsoft company song. Read it and then talk about the questions below.

> Our competitors were laughing, said our network was a fake
> Saw the Internet economy as simply theirs to take
> They'll regret that fateful day
> The sleeping giant did awake
> We embrace and we extend!

1 What event in Microsoft's recent history does the song describe?
2 Do you think that it is motivating for people to look back on a company's past successes?
3 What are the good points about having a company song?
4 How would you feel if your company asked you to sing a song similar to this one?

**MISSION STATEMENTS**

Many modern businesses have mission statements – documents which explain what the company is trying to achieve. Read this mission statement, which was written by the management consultant Eileen Shapiro to show the kind of language that is often used in these documents.

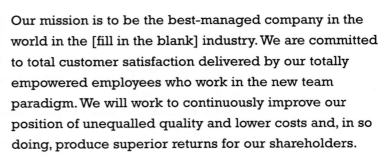

# Mission Statement

> Our mission is to be the best-managed company in the world in the [fill in the blank] industry. We are committed to total customer satisfaction delivered by our totally empowered employees who work in the new team paradigm. We will work to continuously improve our position of unequalled quality and lower costs and, in so doing, produce superior returns for our shareholders.

**1** Which of these sentences most closely describes your first reaction to the mission statement?

- It's typical of many mission statements that I've seen before.
- It's an inspiring and highly motivating document.
- It doesn't really tell us anything about the company's mission at all.
- It's almost completely incomprehensible.

**2** Here, in simpler English, are some of the things expressed in the mission statement above. Match each sentence to a phrase with similar meaning in the text.

> We'll keep our customers happy.
> Our employees will work together.
> We'll make bigger profits.
> Our products will be the cheapest and the best.
> Our employees will take responsibility.

**3** Do you think that the mission statement would be better written in simple English? Why – or why not?

**YOUR MISSION**

Choose a company that you know well. Think of two or three things which you think that company is trying to achieve. Write a short mission statement to motivate its employees. You can make the language as simple or as complicated as you like.

**MOTIVATING AND YOU**

Discuss these questions.

*1* What is the most motivating experience in business that you have had (or that you have heard about)? Why was it effective?

*2* How would you try to motivate your employees?

# issues

## *Management tales*

**AN EXPENSIVE EDUCATION**

**1** 🔊 👥 Listen to this story about how Thomas Watson Senior, the man who built IBM, dealt with a young executive at the company. Summarise the story.

**2** 👥 Discuss these questions.

*1* Would you deal with the young executive in the same way? Why – or why not?

*2* What's the biggest mistake that you've made in your career (in business or in your studies)? How did your boss (or teacher) handle the situation? How would you have handled it differently?

*3* To what extent do you think that mistakes are an important part of the learning process?

👥 Read these three texts and then discuss the questions which follow.

# Kissinger and Winston Lord

Henry Kissinger was the American President Richard Nixon's Secretary of State for Foreign Affairs in the early 1970s. He was famous not just for his ability to manipulate international politics, but also for his ability to control his staff.

One day, he asked a young man called Winston Lord to write a report on a very complicated subject. Lord was new to his job and worked as hard as he could on the report for two weeks before sending it to his boss.

Two days later, the report came back with a note from Kissinger that simply said, 'Is this the best you can do?'

Lord was very worried and worked late for several nights before submitting the report to Kissinger again.

But once more, the report came back with the same brief message, 'Is this really the best you can do?'

Yet again Lord worked long and hard over a new version of the report. When the same note came back from Kissinger again, Lord finally lost patience. He picked up the phone and called his boss. 'Damn it,' he said, 'yes, it's the best I can do.'

Kissinger replied calmly: 'Fine, then I guess I'll read it this time.'

*1* What point do you think Kissinger was trying to make?

*2* How would you react in Winston Lord's position?

*3* What are the good and bad points of Kissinger's management style?

# Rubens' Studio

TOWARDS the end of his career, the great Dutch painter Peter Paul Rubens was receiving so many orders for paintings that he couldn't possibly paint them all himself. So he started to employ other painters to help him. One of these painters specialised in people, another painted clothing, another would work on backgrounds, and so on. In this way, Rubens' studio could work on many pieces at the same time and Rubens could increase his output dramatically.

But whenever a customer came to visit, Rubens would order the other painters to leave and he would work on the paintings alone, with great skill and speed. The customers were amazed by the old man's enormous energy and always went home happy.

*1* In what ways was Rubens' studio like a modern business? Give examples.
*2* Do you think it was right for Rubens to organise his work like this? Explain your views.
*3* Do you think that it is right for modern bosses to receive the credit for the work of others?

## Silent Sloan

Alfred Sloan was the boss of the American car company General Motors at a time when it was the biggest company in the world, with over 750,000 employees. He controlled his huge corporation by having endless meetings with his top managers and listening to opinions from every part of his vast empire.

It is perhaps surprising that Sloan was so keen on attending meetings, because from a fairly early age he had had problems with his hearing. This meant that in meetings he always had to use a big old-fashioned hearing aid. When he wanted to listen to what his managers were saying, he switched his hearing aid on. Before he wanted to speak, he switched it off with a loud click. But this hearing aid was certainly not a disadvantage to him; in fact, it was once called the 'greatest management tool in history'.

*1* In what ways do you think that Sloan's hearing aid could have been a useful management tool?
*2* Can you think of any other examples of managers (or teachers) who have used an unusual personal style to help them in their work?

**MANAGEMENT AND YOU**   What four pieces of advice would you give to a new boss about management? Write them down and then compare your advice with the advice of another pair.

# 4 face to face

**AN EVERYDAY PROBLEM**

In the book *The Greatest Sales Stories Ever Told*, an American woman called Betsy Martin tells this story from her time working as a sales representative for *Money* magazine.

Read the first part of the story and answer these questions.

1 How would you describe Mark Franklin's behaviour?
2 Do you think that Betsy Martin handles the situation in the best way? Explain.
3 In her situation, what action would you take next?

I was getting ready to leave the office when the phone rang. It was Mark Franklin, the management supervisor of my largest account.

Franklin was upset over a discrepancy in his invoice. Before I could get a word in, he began to read the riot act to me.

'I'm sorry, sir, but I don't have any of the details,' I replied. 'Please let me check this and get back to you tomorrow.'

But no matter how reasonable I tried to be, he simply would not stop. Since he represented my biggest account, I wanted to avoid confrontation. However, I drew the line when he began to swear at me.

'If you are going to shout,' I told him, 'you will force me to hang up. If you continue to use that language, we cannot talk.'

The statement was intended to calm him down, or at the very least to break the ice. Unfortunately, it had no such effect!

Finally I told him, 'If you're going to yell at me, at least have the decency to do it to my face. You're only a couple of blocks away. Why don't I come over and we can talk about it?'

'Forget it! I'm too busy!' he snapped back. 'Now, damn it, just take care of it!'

Before I could say a word, I was hearing the dial tone.

**❙ GLOSSARY ❙**

to read the riot act   *to be extremely angry*
to draw the line   *to say that you've had enough*
to swear   *to use bad language*
to yell   *to shout*

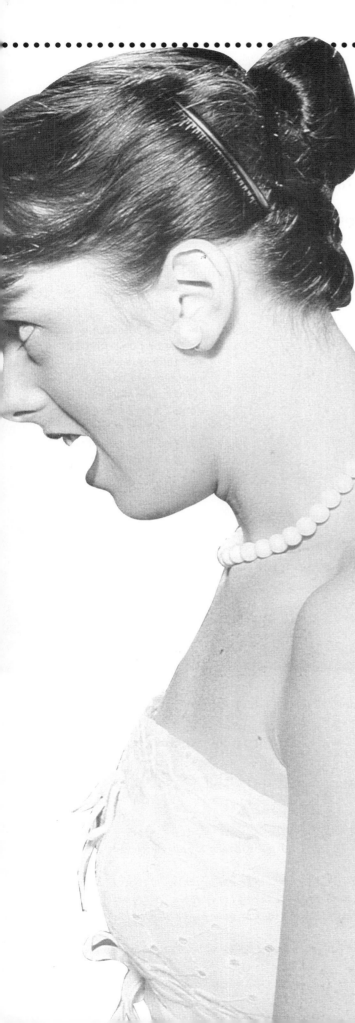

## ANGER AND OFFENCE

Talk about these questions.

1 Have you ever experienced similar behaviour from a customer or a superior? How did you react to it?
2 What business situations do you think make people angry and abusive?
3 Do you think that Franklin would have acted in the same way if he had met Betsy Martin face to face?

## BETSY'S SOLUTION

After a sleepless night, Betsy Martin decided to go to Mark Franklin's office and try to talk to him face to face. Read what happened and then talk about these questions.

1 Do you think that Betsy Martin did the right thing? Why – or why not?
2 Did Franklin react in the way that you thought he would?
3 What are the good points about the way that Betsy Martin handles the situation?

Fortunately he walked by as I was talking to the receptionist on his floor. I caught up with him.

'Mr Franklin,' I said, 'I'm Betsy Martin from *Money*.' He stopped walking and, caught off guard, he seemed much meeker and milder.

'M-m-money?' he stammered. 'Haven't we ...?'

'That's right, sir,' I said as cheerfully as I could. 'I have your file in my briefcase so we can review it.'

'I'm on my way to a ...'

'Now that we've met face to face,' I interrupted, 'maybe we can go over all these troubles with those billing discrepancies. If I caught you at a bad moment, I'll just sit down here in the lobby until you have time.'

'Ms Martin,' he said apologetically, 'won't you please come into my office? I am sure we can resolve this matter.' We walked into his office and he held the door open like a perfect gentleman.

Of course, we got along well. Our meeting was the beginning of a wonderful long-term relationship.

**■ GLOSSARY ■**

off guard   *unprepared*
meeker and milder   *quieter and more timid*
lobby   *the reception area*

## DIFFICULT SITUATIONS AND YOU

Talk about these questions.

1 What do you think – in difficult situations, is it best to deal with people by e-mail, by phone or face to face? Give examples from your own experience.
2 In a face-to-face situation, do you think that it is an advantage or a disadvantage to be a woman in business? Explain.

# GRAMMAR REVIEW

**RUNNING A MEETING**   In an article for *Management Today*, the businessman and writer Winston Fletcher writes about the first impression that most people have of running a meeting.

Read the text and answer these questions.

*1* Why does Winston Fletcher think that, for most people, it comes as a shock to run a meeting?

*2* Do you agree that most business meetings today will have procedures that are less formal than in the past? Give examples.

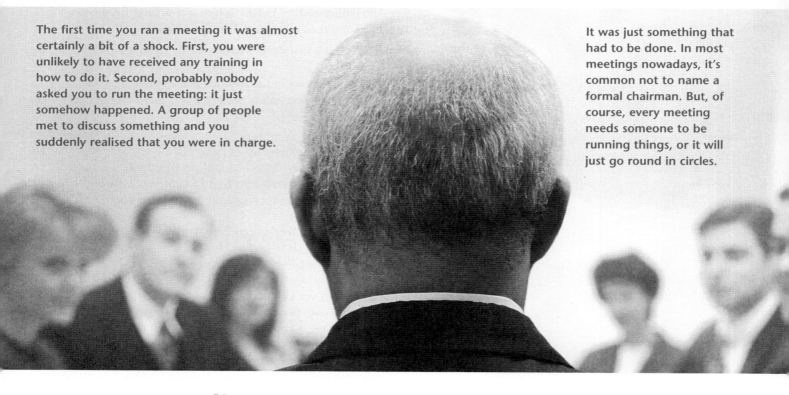

The first time you ran a meeting it was almost certainly a bit of a shock. First, you were unlikely to have received any training in how to do it. Second, probably nobody asked you to run the meeting: it just somehow happened. A group of people met to discuss something and you suddenly realised that you were in charge.

It was just something that had to be done. In most meetings nowadays, it's common not to name a formal chairman. But, of course, every meeting needs someone to be running things, or it will just go round in circles.

**INFINITIVES**   Look at the text again and find examples of these kinds of verbs:

▌a present infinitive      *to do*                        ▌a passive infinitive      *to be done*
▌a negative infinitive      *not to do*                  ▌a continuous infinitive      *to be doing*
▌a past infinitive      *to have done*

▌ *For more on this, see pages 133 and 134.* ▌

**INFINITIVE PRACTICE**   Choose the correct form of the infinitive in these sentences.

*1* Before a meeting starts, people need *to be read / to have read / not to read* all relevant documents.

*2* At the beginning of a meeting, it's important *to state / to be stating / to be stated* its objectives.

*3* During a meeting, it's a good idea for someone *to be taking / to be taken / not to take* notes.

*4* If you want to finish a meeting on time, it's a good idea *to allow / to be allowed / not to allow* people to speak for too long.

*5* At the end of the meeting, the decisions ought *to record / to be recorded / to have recorded*.

# Infinitives and gerunds

**INFINITIVE OR GERUND?**

It can often be difficult to decide when to use the infinitive and when to use the gerund (-*ing* form). Test your knowledge by looking at another passage from Winston Fletcher's article and choosing the correct form of the verbs in italics.

The problems in meetings, as always in management, are people. When you are running a meeting, the following are the most difficult kinds of people to deal with.

### WHISPERERS

These are the ones who chat and giggle with their neighbours. They often seem (1) *to be / being* likeable, but they tend (2) *to irritate / irritating* others in the meeting.

### LOUDMOUTHS

They are the people who shout and try (3) *to bully / bullying* others. They want (4) *to dominate / dominating* the proceedings. If you allow them (5) *to talk / talking* for too long, everyone in the meeting will get frustrated with both them and you.

### INTERRUPTERS

Unfortunately, these are often senior managers who would probably like (6) *to run / running* the meeting themselves. A good meeting leader has to stop them (7) *to interrupt / interrupting* everyone else.

### BROKEN RECORDS

These are the people who keep (8) *to repeat / repeating* the same point over and over again. When you see this (9) *to happen / happening*, it's important to make sure that the meeting doesn't stop (10) *to move / moving* forward.

Chairing meetings is hard work. That's why those who can do it successfully soon get a seat at the manager's top table!

**CHECK**

Some verbs are normally followed by the **infinitive** (e.g. I want *to go* home), while others are normally followed by the **gerund** (e.g. I keep *seeing* him).

However, many common verbs can be followed by either. In certain cases, the use of the infinitive or gerund will change the meaning and in certain cases it won't.

■ *For more on this, see pages 133 and 134.* ■

**MEETINGS AND YOU**

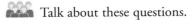 Talk about these questions.

1 Have you had experience in meetings of any of the kinds of people that Winston Fletcher talks about? Tell the story.
2 What other kinds of irritating people would you add to his list? Think of two.
3 Do any people in your class or company fit any of Winston Fletcher's categories?

## Meetings and technology

**TECHNOLOGY AND TRAVEL**

**1** Before you read the article opposite, discuss these questions.

*1* Over the past ten years, there have been many new developments in communications technology. How many can you name?

*2* Would you expect these developments to lead to more or fewer face-to-face meetings? Explain.

*3* What impact would you expect this to have on the airline industry? Explain.

**2** Read section **1** of the article. Do the ideas on the subject surprise you?

**OPPORTUNITIES**

**1** Here are some words from the first section of the article. Which are associated with the appearance, and which with the disappearance, of business opportunities?

*explode*  *shrink*  **vanish**
**obliterate**  *fuel*
*obsolete*  *expansion*  **growth**

**2** Choose the correct form of four of the words above to complete this summary of the first section.

A few years ago, airlines expected their business to (1) _____ , but, in fact, new technology has (2) _____ a huge (3) _____ in demand for their services. This is because the (4) _____ of the Internet has allowed businesses to reach new customers in remote places.

**REASONS FOR MEETING**

Read section **2** of the article and then do the following.

*1* The section lists five reasons why meeting face to face is important. Match each reason to one of the following:

| | |
|---|---|
| making people do what you want | |
| raising money | |
| generating ideas | |
| solving crises | |
| finalising arrangements | |

*2* What other reasons for having a face-to-face meeting can you think of?

**VIDEO-CONFERENCING**

**1** Before you read section **3** , talk about this question.

How do you think video-conferencing would make you feel?

*self-conscious*  *empowered*  *fixated*  **relaxed**
tense  focused  *alienated*  *self-confident*

**2** Read section **3** of the article. Does the business community's opinion of video-conferencing surprise you?

# Face to face or interface?

**1** It wasn't supposed to be this way. Technology was going to shrink and link the world and, in doing so, render one's physical location practically irrelevant. That's why, just a few years ago, the airlines were fretting about the growth of the Internet, e-mail and video-conferencing. The ultimate fear: would business travel become obsolete?

Those worries have vanished into the stratosphere. As the global economy exploded during the past decade, communications technology fuelled the expansion but did not obliterate the need for face-to-face meetings. 'Technology allowed businesses like ours to get customers in remote places where we didn't have a physical presence,' says Dennis DeAndre of LoopNet, a real estate listings site. 'But you still had to get on a plane and go there to really make things happen.'

**2** Indeed, technology serves merely as a starting point in long distance business relationships. To do the hard stuff – closing deals, putting out fires, brainstorming, securing finance, kicking butt – you have to materialize on the spot. So the Net actually has put more people in the air, a phenomenon that might be called Saffo's law.

'If you talk to someone electronically,' explains Paul Saffo, a director of the Institute for the Future in Menlo Park, California, 'it will inevitably lead to a face-to-face meeting.'

**3** Video-conferencing might have prevented all this, but it hasn't, mainly because most people hate it. 'It's a hideous medium,' says the Doblin Group's Joe Crump. 'People become bizarrely self-conscious and unnaturally fixated on the person on TV and less on the people in the room.' Crump's gripe is echoed throughout the business world, along with complaints about delays in transmission and compatibility problems.

'There's no value in a fuzzy picture of people sitting around a conference table,' says T. J. Rodgers, founder of Cypress Semiconductor.

**❙ GLOSSARY ❙**

to fret  *to worry*
to materialize on the spot  *to go to a particular place*
gripe  *complaint*

Wired *Aug 99*

**MEETINGS AND YOU**   **1** Here are some new technologies that allow businesspeople to avoid face-to-face meetings. How would they make you feel?

video phone      conference call      Web discussion group

**2** How important do you think that face-to-face business meetings will be in the future?

# doing **business** 1 *Tough meetings*

**OZWALD BOATENG**  Read this story about the British fashion designer Ozwald Boateng and answer the questions below.

# A Tough Meeting

In the 1990s, Ozwald Boateng was one of the rising stars of the fashion industry. His stylish suits and colourful shirts were worn by top businesspeople and politicians, as well as celebrities like Mick Jagger and George Michael. He was also greatly admired for his business acumen, and by the time he was in his early thirties he had four companies with a turnover of more than £3 million. But then things started to go badly wrong. A financial crisis in the Far East threw one of his main markets into turmoil and, unexpectedly, some of his biggest customers cancelled orders worth over £1 million. The effect on Boateng's business was disastrous. He now found that he had huge debts and no means of paying them off. He realised that he had no choice: he had to call in the receivers.

The meeting with the receivers was the toughest one of Boateng's career. He knew that they would normally try to pay off a business's debts by selling its assets, but in this case the main asset of the business was Boateng himself. So what would they do? After some discussion, they decided that the only thing to do was to sell his own business back to him. 'Right, let's get this over with, Boateng,' they said. 'Get out your cheque book.' 'But I haven't got any money,' he replied. Then, thinking quickly, he asked, 'Can you lend it to me?' 'You must be joking,' they said …

### ▌ GLOSSARY ▌

acumen *the ability to think and judge quickly and well*

receivers *people who are put in charge of a company in cases of business failure or bankruptcy*

to throw into turmoil *to cause confusion and trouble*

1  Why did Boateng's business fail?

2  Why couldn't the receivers sell Boateng's assets?

3  Why do you think the receivers call him 'Boateng' and not 'Ozwald' or 'Mr Boateng'?

4  In Ozwald Boateng's situation, what would you say next? (To find out what happened, turn to page 125.)

*Ozwald Boateng*

**SETTING THE TONE**

**1** The receivers speak to Boateng in a very direct way. Look at the text again and find phrases with a similar meaning to the phrases in the table.

|  | POLITE | DIRECT |
|---|---|---|
| Getting to the point | Shall we get down to business? |  |
| Asking for money | How would you like to pay? |  |
| Refusing | That could be hard to arrange. |  |

**2** Here are six more phrases that you might hear in meetings – three polite and three direct. Write the numbers in the correct spaces in the table below.

1 *I'm not sure I'm with you on this point.*

2 Could you just run through that again?

3 *Can we stick to the point?*

4 **That's not what I wanted to hear.**

5 **So what exactly are you saying?**

6 Shall we get back to the main subject?

|  | POLITE | DIRECT |
|---|---|---|
| Asking for clarification |  |  |
| Disagreeing |  |  |
| Controlling digressions |  |  |

**TOUGH ROLES**

Use the role cards on page 125 (Student **A**) and page 126 (Student **B**) to role play the first minute or so of two meetings. You can use tactics similar to the ones above or others that you think may be more effective.

47

# doing business 2  *Answering questions*

**THE IRON LADY**
The former British Prime Minister Margaret Thatcher was famous for her ability to answer any question. You will hear part of a TV interview she gave in the early 1980s, a time of very high unemployment in the UK. The interviewer asks her: 'Will we ever return to full employment?'

Listen to what she says in reply and answer these questions.

1   What is Margaret Thatcher's first answer to the question?
2   She talks about three periods of business development – what does she call each of these three periods?
3   In each of the three periods she says that people had the same reaction – what was it?
4   Do you think that she gives a satisfactory answer to the interviewer's question? Why – or why not?

**A STRAIGHT ANSWER**
A straight answer is one which tries to give the kind of information or opinions that the questioner wants. Business communication experts suggest this formula for 'straight' answers.

| ANSWER | + | REASON | + | EXAMPLE |
|---|---|---|---|---|
| The facts or the point that you want to make. | | Your explanation for your answer. Start with: *That's because ... / The reason for this is ...* | | A short example or story to illustrate what you have said. Start with: *For example, ... / For instance, ...* |

**1**   Listen to a different answer to the same question about unemployment that you heard Margaret Thatcher answer. It uses the answer–reason–example formula. Answer these questions.

1   What's the answer?
2   What's the reason?
3   What's the example?

**2**   Listen again to Mrs Thatcher's answer to the question about unemployment. To what extent do you think that she used this formula?

**YOUR STRAIGHT ANSWERS**
**1**   Take turns to ask and answer these questions. The person answering should try to use the answer–reason–example formula whenever possible.

▍ Do you believe that you are ready to do business in English?
▍ What's the best way of travelling from your home town to New York?
▍ Do you think that businesspeople should have laptop or desktop computers?
▍ Do you think that most managers spend too much time in meetings?

**2**   Think of at least two of your own questions and do the same as above.

**Q = A + 1**  When answering questions from journalists, the former American President Ronald Reagan used this formula to make sure that he got his point across.

| Q | = | A | + | 1 |
|---|---|---|---|---|
| QUESTION | | ANSWER | CONTROL PHRASE | YOUR POINT |
| | | a brief answer | a link phrase | the thing you really want to say |

On the recording you'll hear answers given to these three questions:

*Ronald Reagan*

> Can you explain why the company is planning to shut down another factory at the end of next month?

SHAREHOLDER

> Is it true that everyone in your department was out at lunch for over three hours last Friday?

MANAGER

> Why has the government again decided to increase taxes on fuel, when businesses have been asking for a reduction in these rates for years?

JOURNALIST

**1** Listen to the three answers and make a note of the following.

*1* What is the brief answer to each question?
*2* What is the point that each person really wants to make?

**2** Listen again and make a note of the three 'control phrases' that are used to link the two parts of the answers together.

**A + 1 ROLES**  Take turns to ask and answer these questions. The person answering should try to use the Q = A + 1 formula.

▌**A** You are a journalist who wants to know whether a recent rail crash was due to lack of investment by a private rail company.
**B** You are the director of the private rail company and, although it's true that investment in safety has been below target, you want to tell people that your company has the best safety record in the industry.

▌**B** You are a customer who wants to know why your delivery of goods is late for the second month in a row.
**A** You are **B**'s supplier. You admit that there have been some problems at your warehouse, but you want to say that you still offer the most efficient service and the lowest prices in the country.

For more roles, use the role cards on page 125 (Student **A**) and page 126 (Student **B**).

**THATCHER AGAIN**  Listen to another TV interview that Margaret Thatcher gave in the 1980s. The interviewer asks her if she thinks that the idea of popular capitalism has become a bit 'tattered' – or old and worn out.

*1* What is Thatcher's answer to the question?
*2* Why do you think that the interviewer interrupts Mrs Thatcher when he does?
*3* What does this tell you about his interviewing technique?

# issues

## *Under pressure*

**FEELING THE PRESSURE**

Discuss these questions.

1 Which of these situations do you find the most pressurised?

▮ speaking in front of a large group of people
▮ attending a large meeting
▮ having a one-to-one interview
▮ taking a big decision

2 What other parts of business life do you find pressurised?

3 What happens to you when you're under pressure?

**BUSINESS AND SPORT**

Will Carling is a successful business consultant who was also a top international sportsman. Read what he wrote about success in business and success in sport and answer the questions.

1 What comparison does he make between business and sport?

2 What signs of pressure does he say are acceptable?

3 What does he say that businesspeople and athletes should try to avoid?

4 Do you think that 'grace under pressure' is a good definition of courage? What other definitions can you think of?

### The Way To Win

To non-athletes, the pressure of the putt that will win or lose the Open, the penalty that will win or lose the Grand Slam, the serve on which the vital Wimbledon tie-break depends, seems impossibly severe. To the champion, it is just one more test of skill, concentration and preparation.

Managers need the same mental conditioning to generate the courage to make their decisions and take the actions they know to be right. Once doubt creeps in, for athletes and managers alike, the courage falters: the kick, the serve, the putt, the business opportunity are missed. 'Grace under pressure' is almost a definition of courage. It doesn't mean having nerves of steel. The greatest sportsman can suffer extreme nervousness before the event. That's part of the adrenalin build-up that produces peak performance, and is in no way a sign of weakness.

*Will Carling – England's most successful rugby union captain of all time.*

▮ **GLOSSARY** ▮

putt    *the shot a golfer makes to put the ball into the hole*

Grand Slam    *the highest honour in Europe's main international rugby championship*

grace    *fairness and decency*

**PREPARING FOR PRESSURE**

Discuss these questions.

*1* How do you compose yourself before a key moment in life? Here are a few suggestions.

▌ Empty your mind of all thoughts and distractions.
▌ Breathe deeply and relax.
▌ Remember your most successful previous experience.
▌ Visualise success in the experience that you're facing.

*2* What has been the most pressurised moment in your life? How did you prepare for it? If you had to face the experience again, what would you do differently?

**SPORTING COMPARISONS**

**1** Can you think of a situation in business life which is similar to each of these sporting situations? In each case, what lessons can businesspeople learn from the sporting comparison?

*a ski jumper taking off*

*a pitstop*

*arguing with the umpire*

*a footballer being sent off*

**2** What other parallels between the worlds of business and sport can you think of?

# 5 risk and reward

**THE RECIPE FOR SUCCESS**

 Talk about the following.

1 What qualities do you think that people need to be successful in business? Rank the words in the box from 1 (high) to 9 (low).

| | | |
|---|---|---|
| honesty | talent | persistence |
| courage | education | luck |
| genius | toughness | charm |

2 Decide on two other qualities which are important for success. Where would they come in your list?

3 Compare your lists with the rest of the class.

**THE WISDOM OF COOLIDGE**

Calvin Coolidge was president of the USA in the 1920s. His words about the reasons for success have been regularly quoted by businesspeople ever since that time.

 Read Coolidge's text and then talk about these questions.

1 How different are Calvin Coolidge's ideas from yours? Which parts of the text do you disagree with?

2 In what ways has the recipe for success changed since Coolidge's time?

Nothing in the world can take the place of persistence.

Talent will not; nothing is more common than unsuccessful people with talent.

Genius will not; unrewarded genius is almost a proverb.

Education will not; the world is full of educated derelicts.

Persistence and determination alone are omnipotent.

The slogan *press on* has solved and always will solve the problems of the human race.

**┃ GLOSSARY ┃**

derelicts *homeless people, tramps*
omnipotent *all powerful*
press on *keep going*

**REWARD**

 Discuss these questions.

1 Do you think that 'persistence' should be more highly rewarded financially than the other qualities that Coolidge mentions?

2 Look back at the list you made earlier. Which qualities would you like to see more highly rewarded by society?

**PROFIT
AND
PLANTS**

 Read this text and discuss the questions below.

One day, Swedish artist Ola Pehrson decided to turn her yucca plant into a financial speculator. She placed sensors on the plant's leaves which could detect changes in its electrical activity. A computer program then translated these electrical changes into decisions to buy or sell shares on the Stockholm Stock Exchange.

The plant was competing against some of the brightest and most highly paid people on the world's financial markets, but at the end of three months it had still managed to produce a healthy 18% return on Ms Pehrson's investment.

1 What does the story of Ola Pehrson's yucca plant tell you about the behaviour of the financial markets?
2 What does it tell you about the people that make their fortunes from them?

**RISK** **1** Talk about what you would do in these situations. Which of you, do you think, is the bigger risk taker?

While running a large project for your company, you realise that you have made a mistake and overspent your budget by 30%. Do you admit that you have made the mistake immediately? Do you decide to save an equivalent amount on a future project and then put the situation back into balance? Or do you simply start applying for new jobs and hope you get one before you are found out?

You want to buy a new car that costs $10,000 and so far you have saved $1,000. A close friend owns a racehorse and tells you that he is certain that it will win its next race. The betting odds on the horse are 10 to 1. Do you bet any money on the horse – and if so, how much?

You own 1,000 shares in a medium-sized company that runs pizza restaurants around the world. One Friday there are rumours that the CEO and founder of the company has decided to resign. As a result, the share price falls by 15%.
You have the weekend to decide what to do with your shares. Will you sell them first thing on Monday morning? Will you wait and see if the rumours are true before deciding? Or will you ignore the present situation and assume that things will be OK in the long term?

**2** Who is the biggest risk taker you know of? Tell the story.

# G R A M M A R   R E V I E W

**MOSAIC**

*Marc Andreessen*

■ **CHECK**

**Relative clauses** either help to define words in the main part of the sentence or add information to it.

■ *For more on relative clauses, see page 144.* ■

These two pages tell the story of Marc Andreessen and Jim Clark, and the founding of Netscape.

**1** Listen to the first part of the Netscape story and fill the gaps in the text.

> In early 1994, when Marc Andreessen was just twenty-three years old, he arrived in California's Silicon Valley with an idea (1) _____ . As a student at the University of Illinois, he and his friends had developed a program called Mosaic, (2) _____ .
> Before Mosaic, the Web had been used mainly by scientists and other technical people (3) _____ . But with Mosaic, Andreessen and his friends had developed a program (4) _____ .
> Mosaic was an overnight success. It was put on the university's network at the beginning of 1993 and by the end of the year it had over a million users.
> But Andreessen was frustrated. Although he and his friends had done all the work to develop Mosaic, it was his bosses at the university (5) _____ .
> So, in early 1994, Andreessen left the University of Illinois, (6) _____ , and went to seek his fortune in Silicon Valley.

**2** Compare your answers with a partner and listen again to check.

**3** How successful do you think the Internet would be today if it didn't have pictures?

**ANDREESSEN AND CLARK**

*Jim Clark*

**1** Look at the next part of the Netscape story and use relative clauses to join each group of sentences together to make one long sentence. For example:

California's most dynamic business is the computer industry. It is centred on an area just outside San Francisco.

*California's most dynamic business is the computer industry, which is centred on an area just outside San Francisco.*

*1* Soon after Andreessen arrived in Silicon Valley, he started to have meetings with a man called Jim Clark. He was one of the Valley's most famous entrepreneurs.

*2* Clark had founded a company called Silicon Graphics. It produced big computer systems. They were used by Hollywood film studios as well as aircraft and car designers.

*3* In early 1994, nobody was making any real money from the Internet. It was still very slow and hard to use.

*4* But Andreessen had seen an opportunity. It would make him and Clark rich men within two years.

*5* He suggested they should create a new computer program. It would do the same job as Mosaic but would be much easier to use.

*6* He pointed out that the Internet would soon have over fifty million users. They would all be potential customers for their idea.

*7* Clark listened carefully to Andreessen. His ideas and enthusiasm impressed him greatly.

*8* Eventually, Clark agreed to invest $3 million of his own money in the project and to raise an extra $15 million from venture capitalists. They were always keen to listen to Clark's new ideas.

# *Relative clauses*

**Search**

**Home**

**Print**

**Back**

2  Compare your answers with a partner and then check by listening to the second part of the story.

3  In industries based on computers and the Internet, do you think it is easier for very young people to raise money than for people with more business experience? Give examples.

**THE BIRTH OF NETSCAPE**

1  Read the final part of the Netscape story. In each sentence, find a relative clause that can be shortened to make it sound more natural. For example:

Clark, ~~who was~~ helped by a number of professional managers, organised the financial side of the company.

Andreessen's team, ~~which consisted~~ *consisting* of many of his old university friends, were totally committed to the project.

*1*  Clark and Andreessen decided to call their new company Netscape, and soon their offices were full of young software engineers who were working day and night to complete the new program.

*2*  In October 1994, Netscape launched its new browser, which was called Navigator, and by the following summer it had over ten million users.

*3*  The success of the Netscape Navigator persuaded Clark that they should offer shares for sale to the general public, which would allow the company to raise a great deal of extra money.

*4*  When Netscape's shares went on sale in August 1995, their value increased by three times in just one day, which made it the most successful share offer in history.

*5*  The Netscape shares which were owned by the company's two founders had made them rich beyond their wildest dreams: Jim Clark had become a billionaire and Marc Andreessen, at the age of just twenty-four, was worth over $80 million.

2  Compare your answers with a partner and then listen to the last part of the story.

**CHECK**

You can sometimes replace the relative pronoun and verb in an active relative clause with the present participle.

If the verb in the relative clause is passive, use the past participle.

**START-UPS AND YOU**  Talk about these questions.

*1*  Do you think that the huge sums of money raised by Internet start-ups like Netscape, Yahoo!, Amazon and e-bay were justified?

*2*  In what circumstances would you invest money in businesses which had no proven record of making profits?

## Investment

**TRADER OR BROKER?**  In the USA in recent years, there has been a big change in the way that people invest money. Before reading about this in the article opposite, combine the words in the two boxes to make phrases which match the definitions on the right. (A trader is someone who buys and sells; a broker is a person who buys and sells for someone else.)

> stock  day
> online
>
> trader  broker

- a person or company which buys and sells shares for someone else
- an ordinary person who buys and sells shares for him or herself
- an ordinary person who buys and sells shares through the Internet
- a person who offers services to allow people to buy and sell shares on the Internet
- a person who uses the Internet to buy and sell shares for him or herself in a single day

**THE REVOLUTION**  Read section **1** of the text and do the following.

*1* Find phrases with a similar meaning to the phrases in the box. Can you think of any other ways of saying them?

*2* How would you summarise the way that investment in America is changing?

> for richer or for poorer
> ordinary people like you and me
> from the New York Stock market
>   to small town America

**THEN AND NOW**

**1**  Before you read section **2**, match the underlined words to these definitions.

- a collection of shares in different companies
- a situation in which business is controlled by one company or institution
- a company that invests money in the stocks and shares of many different businesses for small investors.
- a percentage of the value of a deal paid to the person who handles it
- the power to take a decision

**2**  Now read section **2** and answer these questions.

*1* Why did individual investors get a bad deal in the old days?
*2* What was the social change that led to change in the financial services industry?
*3* What major technological change revolutionised financial services?

**3**  Explain in your own words what these phrases mean.

> you paid through the nose
>       the main event
>
> the cracks began
> to appear

**INVESTMENT AND YOU**  Read section **3** and then discuss the following.

*1* Apart from the ones mentioned here, what other online financial services have you used or heard about?
*2* How would you prefer to spend your free time – investing your money or gardening?
*3* Has this American way of investing become popular in your country? If it hasn't, do you think it will in future?

# A nation of TRADERS

**1**

There's a revolution underway and it's changing the way we invest and work and live. Our money is no longer with some broker or fund manager. Our money is with ourselves. For better or for worse, we are fast becoming a nation of stock traders. And while it's easy to get caught up in all the fuss about day traders and Internet IPOs, the real story runs much deeper than that. Power that for generations lay with a few thousand white males in New York City is now being seized by Everyman and Everywoman. In fact, the movement from Wall Street to Main Street is one of the most significant trends of the past few decades.

*A meeting of a modern American investment club*

**2**

For much of the nation's history, Wall Street has had a <u>monopoly</u> on all facets of the capital markets. It controlled not only the financing of America's companies but also the investments of individuals. Stocks? First of all very few Americans owned them. Those that did had accounts with brokers who managed <u>portfolios</u> with almost complete <u>discretion</u>. They told us when to buy and sell. As for <u>commissions</u>, well, they simply weren't discussed! You paid through the nose and accepted it. But then cracks began to appear. As increasing numbers of Americans joined the middle- and upper-middle classes, demand for financial services soared and competitive pricing entered the picture. <u>Mutual fund</u> companies began offering low cost, diversified portfolios that anyone with $1,000 in his pocket could buy. And now comes the main event. I'm talking of course about online trading. It's here. It's real. And it's growing fast. The Internet!

**3**

The attraction of online trading is obvious. With the click of a mouse, through any one of scores of online brokers, you can buy and sell any stock anywhere in the world, day or night. There are online banks and online business news services. In fact an entire parallel e-universe of financial services has opened for business. Meanwhile, back in the material world, all sorts of businesses are booming. Investment books are flying off the bookstore shelves. Investing clubs now exceed gardening clubs in popularity by more than four to one!

▌ **GLOSSARY** ▌

Internet IPOs   *initial public offerings that allow*
  *people to buy shares in new Internet companies*
facets   *aspects*
scores of   *lots of*   (a score = 20)

Fortune 11.10.99

*A stockbroker
in the 1950s*

# doing business 1 *Reading share prices*

**BIG NUMBERS**  **1** Match the following to the numbers on the right.

| | |
|---|---|
| the dollar value of Netscape just after its shares had gone on sale to the public for the first time | 180,000 |
| the number of Americans who are worth over $10 million | 80,000,000 |
| the amount of money traded each day on the world's currency markets (in dollars) | 2,700,000,000 |
| Marc Andreessen's wealth at the age of twenty-four (in dollars) | 1,000,000,000,000 |

**2** Say the numbers above, using the guide below to help you if necessary.

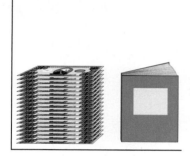

A million has six zeroes.
$1 million in $100 bills would make a stack just over 20cm high.

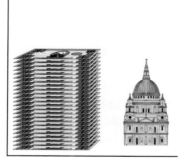

A billion is a thousand million.
$1 billion in $100 bills would be taller than London's St Paul's cathedral.

A trillion is a million million.
$1 trillion in $100 bills would make a stack 190km high, 20 times higher than Mount Everest!

**SHARE PRICES** This is how the *Financial Times* presents information about companies' share prices. In this case it shows details of shares at the end of the first week of the millennium for the company that owns the famous Selfridges department store.

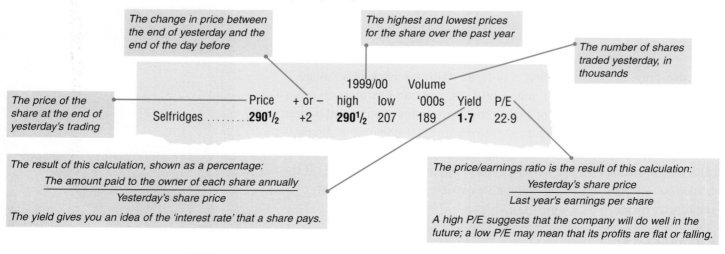

The change in price between the end of yesterday and the end of the day before

The highest and lowest prices for the share over the past year

The number of shares traded yesterday, in thousands

The price of the share at the end of yesterday's trading

| | Price | + or − | 1999/00 high | low | Volume '000s | Yield | P/E |
|---|---|---|---|---|---|---|---|
| Selfridges | 290¹/₂ | +2 | 290¹/₂ | 207 | 189 | 1·7 | 22·9 |

The result of this calculation, shown as a percentage:
$$\frac{\text{The amount paid to the owner of each share annually}}{\text{Yesterday's share price}}$$
The yield gives you an idea of the 'interest rate' that a share pays.

The price/earnings ratio is the result of this calculation:
$$\frac{\text{Yesterday's share price}}{\text{Last year's earnings per share}}$$
A high P/E suggests that the company will do well in the future; a low P/E may mean that its profits are flat or falling.

If you were interested in buying shares in Selfridges tomorrow, which of these figures would you be most interested in? Explain why.

**BUSINESS VOICES**

Listen to two investors talking about how they use financial information about shares.

**1** Tom Hawkings is a City of London stockbroker. Listen to what he says and answer the questions.

*1* Which of the share price statistics does he consider most significant?
*2* Which statistic would he look at if he wanted an investment to give him an income?
*3* He talks about volatility – things changing suddenly or dramatically. Which statistic is an indication of this?
*4* Which statistic is an indication of activity?

**2** Listen to Janet Brooks, a venture capitalist, and answer the questions.

*1* What two factors does she think are most important when looking at share prices?
*2* When is the P/E ratio important to her?
*3* When does she try to buy shares in a company?

**WEEK ONE**

At the end of the first week of the twenty-first century, this was the position for the shares of five companies which own some of the UK's most famous High Street shops.

FINANCIAL TIMES  WEEKEND JANUARY 8/JANUARY 9 2000

## LONDON SHARE SERVICE

**GENERAL RETAILERS**

| | Price | + or – | 1999/00 high | low | Volume '000s | Yield | P/E |
|---|---|---|---|---|---|---|---|
| Body Shop | 115 | | 138½ | 77½ | 8 | 5.0 | 36.7 |
| Boots | 636 | +25 | 1030 | 535 | 4,736 | 3.8 | 16.4 |
| Dixons | 1300 | −13 | 1590 | 795 | 3,894 | 1.2 | 33.9 |
| Marks & Spencer | 307³/₄ | +9½ | 472½ | 227 | 24,479 | 4.7 | 28.0 |
| Smith (WH) | 458½ | +6½ | 792½ | 352 | 177 | 4.0 | 12.3 |

 Answer these questions.

*1* Which share had the best day on the market yesterday?
*2* Which share had the worst day?
*3* Which share has the highest yield?
*4* Which company does the market think will do best in future?
*5* If you could buy one of these shares, which one would you buy?

**THE MARKET TODAY**

 Talk about these questions.

*1* Do you know what has happened to any of the companies mentioned above since the first week of 2000? If so, tell the story.
*2* Find a recent newspaper and compare the information about the five companies above at the end of the first week of 2000 to the information given now. How have things changed?

# doing **business 2** *Raising money*

**STARTING A BUSINESS**

**1** If you wanted to start a new business, where would you go for the money that you needed?

*to a bank?*

*to a local businessperson or company?*

**to family or friends?**

**to a stock market?**

**2** Can you think of any other sources of money for new businesses?

**SILICON VALLEY**

According to the writer Michael Lewis in his book *The New New Thing*, this is how Silicon Valley entrepreneur Jim Clark raised money for his new company, Healtheon.

Read the text and talk about the questions below.

NEW COMPANIES are sold to the public in much the same spirit as new books, new music and new politicians. The sellers leap onto airplanes and fly to many cities where they put on a show for the perfect strangers who they hope will buy their product. In the case of a new company, the strangers are money managers and the show is called 'the road show'.

The Healtheon road show had the same two stages as most road shows for Silicon Valley companies. The first stage was in Europe. Europe was a useful place to open not because it had a lot of managers dying to invest in new technology companies but because it didn't. Europeans were famously clueless about new things.

**■ GLOSSARY ■**

| | |
|---|---|
| money managers | *people who manage investments for others* |
| to open | *to start* |
| clueless | *ignorant* |

*Jim Clark and the Healtheon road show*

*1* Does a 'road show' sound like a good way of raising money? Why – or why not?
*2* Why was Europe a good place for the road show to open?
*3* Do you think that people in the USA know more about 'new things' than people in other parts of the world? Give examples.

**BUSINESS MODELS**  People who are starting new businesses often talk about 'business models' – which simply means where the profit is likely to come from. Look at these examples of business models and then discuss the questions below.

> Book publishers make their profit from a book's cover price – the money that people pay to buy the book.

> The cover price of a magazine often doesn't meet the costs of producing it – think how much the glossy pictures and star names cost! Instead, magazine publishers generate profit from the advertising that appears inside their publications.

> Some software companies give their software to individuals for free but charge when businesses want to use their programs.

> Other software companies sell their software at a price that makes them no profit. Instead, they make their money by selling services like technical support and training.

1 Can you think of examples of other kinds of business that have similar business models?
2 What other business models do you know of? Explain how they work.

**BUSINESS PLANS**  A business plan is a document that is produced by a new company that wants to raise money. It will normally contain details of what is to be sold, projected sales and costs, and why the plan will make money. There are no fixed rules for writing business plans, but the left-hand column below lists six sections that you will often see in this kind of document.

Match the sections in the left-hand column with the definitions on the right.

Summary — what might go wrong and what you will do in that situation

Background — a description of your business environment, your main competitors and your customers

Market — the current financial position of your business

Trading summary — the amount of money you want and an explanation of why you need it

Proposal — the history of the business sector that you're planning to enter

Risk — a brief outline of the most important points in your plan

**BUSINESS PLANS AND YOU**  Look at this summary from a business plan and do the following.
1 Make a note of the kind of information that is needed to fill the gaps.
2 Think of an idea for a new business that you could start and then fill the gaps in the summary.
3 Compare your plans with another group. Identify the strengths and weaknesses of each other's plans.

## SUMMARY

We plan to create a new world-class business in the field of (1) ____ . In the first year, we aim to (2) ____ , and in the second year we will (3) ____ . Our main market will be (4) ____ , but our products/services will also appeal to (5) ____ .

We are looking to raise (6) ____ to fund (7) ____ . Within (8) ____ years, we will be able to realise an increase in value of (9) ____ , assuming that (10) ____ .

# issues
## *Fat cats*

**INTRODUCTION**   The pay for the bosses and top executives of large companies has risen dramatically over recent years. But are these 'fat cats' really worth the money that they take home?

**THE AMERICAN VIEW**   This is part of a special report on executive pay by the American magazine, *Business Week*. Read the article and then discuss these questions.

1  Does the level of executive pay in the USA surprise you? Does it seem very different from the situation in your country?
2  Is the comparison between American business and business in the rest of the world a fair one?
3  What arguments in favour of high levels of pay for executives does the article give? Do they convince you? Why – or why not?

## Executive Pay

The stock market has made many people wildly wealthy, and none more so than chief executives at major US companies. Thanks to a pay structure that has linked most executive compensation to the stock market, the head of a large public company made an average $10.6 million in 1998. That's a 36% hike over 1997 – and an astounding 442% increase over the average paycheck of $2 million pocketed in 1990.

But if the numbers are staggering, so too has been the performance of American business. While tradition-bound Europe struggles to boost growth and entrepreneurialism, debt-soaked Japan remains mired in recession and much of the developing world fights to regain its economic footing, US executives are energizing older companies and creating new ones daily. The obvious questions: Are the sky-high pay and the sky-high performance linked? Has pay for performance worked? Is CEO greed good?

Supporters of today's compensation system say this performance is no coincidence. If paying top dollar is the price of ensuring that the boss makes the moves that benefit all investors, fine. The CEOs who have responded to the challenge have created billions in value. And those who fail are pushed out far more quickly – albeit with golden parachutes.

**▌ GLOSSARY ▌**

hike   *increase*
to be mired in   *to be stuck (in a bad situation)*
to pay top dollar   *to pay the highest price*
golden parachute   *a sum of money paid to an executive when he or she leaves a company*

Business Week *19.3.99*

**MORE JUSTIFICATIONS**   Good performance is not the only justification for high earnings. Here are four other possible justifications.

- ▌ to acknowledge exceptional talent
- ▌ to encourage people to take risks
- ▌ to reward contributions to society in general
- ▌ to compensate for sacrifices that a person has made

Discuss these questions.

1  Can you think of any jobs or professions in which earnings are at a high level for any of the above reasons?
2  Could any of these reasons be used to justify the high levels of executive pay?
3  Can you add any reasons to the list?

**ARE THEY WORTH IT?** These people are some of the world's biggest earners in their fields.

*1* How would you justify the amount of money that they earn?
*2* Which ones do you think are worth it?

Compare your ideas with others in the class.

# Anthony Robbins

*Anthony Robbins is an American guru who specialises in helping people to achieve their peak performance. With fees of over $75,000 per day, it's estimated that he makes over $50 million a year from his books and seminars.*

# Tiger Woods

*In 1999, a time when he was considered to be the best golfer in the world, Tiger Woods earned $7.5 million in prize money, and a great deal more from advertising and endorsements.*

*As CEO of Computer Associates International, Charles B. Wang made $670 million in 1999. Much of this sum was paid as a bonus for helping the company's share price achieve its target for the year.*

# Charles B Wang

*In August 1992 the financial speculator George Soros made $1 billion in a single day when he gambled on the British pound sterling leaving the European Exchange Rate Mechanism.*

# George Soros

# Julia Roberts

*With a career that includes films such as* Pretty Woman *and* Notting Hill, *Julia Roberts is probably Hollwood's best paid female star, earning around $17 million for each film.*

# Margaret Whitman

*Margaret Whitman, Chief Executive Officer of the Web auction site e-bay, earned $24.7 million in her first year in the job.*

**PAY AND YOU**  Talk about the following.

The average American boss earns over 400 times as much as the average American worker. If you were the boss of a large successful company, how much more than your workers would you expect to earn? Explain your decision.

# 6 persuasion

**COMMERCIAL MESSAGES**

 It has been estimated that people in the world's richest countries are exposed to around 1,600 commercial messages every day – about one every minute! Where do these commercial messages come from? Make a list of sources and then compare your list with the rest of the class.

**PRODUCT PLACEMENT**

 Read this text and talk about the questions below.

When you watch a TV programme or a movie, you expect to see advertisements in the commercial breaks, but you are also probably receiving a large number of commercial messages during the film or programme as well, thanks to a marketing technique called 'product placement'.

For example, why do the 'men in black' wear Ray-Ban sunglasses? The answer is that Ray-Ban did a deal with the film's producers and followed it with a $10 million advertising campaign.

1 Can you think of any other kinds of product which are promoted in this way through films or TV? (Remember, if a product is mentioned or shown clearly in a modern movie, it's almost certainly not an accident!)
2 If you were a film director, would you be happy with product placement in your movie? Why – or why not?

**ENDORSEMENT**

 Read this text and talk about the questions below.

Many advertisers ask famous, glamorous or successful people to give their approval to particular brands or products – a technique known as endorsement.

After the end of her marriage to the UK's Duke of York, Sarah 'Fergie' Ferguson was asked by the American company WeightWatchers to appear in an advertising campaign for their range of slimming methods and products.

1 Why do you think that WeightWatchers chose Fergie? Do you think she was a good choice? Why – or why not?
2 Think of some other examples of famous people endorsing products. How effective is this technique in persuading you to buy?

**SUPERMARKET STRATEGIES**

Marketing people and advertisers are experts at making people aware of products, but persuading people to buy them is a different skill. Here are some of the ways that supermarkets persuade their customers to buy the products on their shelves.

Read the article and talk about these questions.

1 Which of these sales strategies have you noticed at supermarkets in your country?
2 Do you think that these strategies are effective, or are they irritating?
3 Do you think that any of these sales strategies are unethical?

**DON'T BE DECEIVED.** Shopping at a large modern supermarket might seem a fairly simple experience, but the reality is very different.

A typical large supermarket offers around 17,000 to 20,000 items for sale and it wants to make sure that its customers see as many of them as possible. That's why you'll normally find essential goods like bread, vegetables and meat in completely different parts of the store. Products with a high profit margin are always placed on shelves within easy reach of the customer, while lower margin items, like sugar or flour, are on the top or bottom shelves.

Many people make shopping lists before they visit supermarkets, but even so around 60% of all supermarket purchases are the result of decisions that are taken in the store. For this reason, supermarkets try to tempt their customers by placing certain kinds of products next to each other. In the UK, beer will often be found next to baby's nappies, because research shows that fathers of young children buy nappies on their way home from work and will buy beer at the same time. Research has also shown that this kind of 'impulse buy' happens much more frequently when no sales assistants are nearby – which is why there are often not many assistants available to help customers with purchases.

And have you ever noticed the wonderful smell of fresh bread in supermarkets? Of course, most supermarkets bake bread in the mornings, but the smell of fresh bread has such a positive effect on sales that some of them pump the smell into their air conditioning systems in the afternoons and evenings as well, just to keep their checkouts busy.

In fact, supermarkets have made selling such a fine art that their customers often lose all sense of time. When interviewed, customers will normally guess that they have only spent half an hour in the supermarket, even when they have been there for well over forty-five minutes. But that shouldn't be too surprising. Any really profitable supermarket knows that it should keep its clocks well hidden.

## PERSUASION AND YOU

Talk about these questions.

1 What role did advertising, marketing or sales play in your last purchasing decision?
2 When was the last time that you were persuaded to buy something that you didn't really want? Tell the story.

## G R A M M A R   R E V I E W

**ARALDITE** The adverts on these pages were all included in the best 100 posters of the twentieth century by the advertising trade journal, *Campaign*. This British advert for Araldite glue was the first time that a billboard was used as a three-dimensional medium.

1 Look at the advert and then answer these questions. In each case, explain why.
   1 If you didn't already know about Araldite, what would this poster tell you about the company and its products?
   2 If you use Araldite to stick a handle on a teapot, what kind of result do you think you'll get?
   3 Will people fear for their lives if they walk under this billboard?
   4 How would the advertisers feel if the car fell off?
   5 What changes would you make to this advert, if it were used in your country?

2 Which of the questions above use the first conditional and which use the second conditional? Can you explain why?

### ▌ CHECK

The **first conditional** talks about a realistic condition and its probable result.

*If Araldite sticks a car to a poster, it'll certainly stick a handle to a teapot.*

The **second conditional** talks about a hypothetical condition and its probable result.

*If the car fell off, the advertisers would feel pretty silly.*

▌ *For more on these conditionals, turn to page 129.* ▌

## *Conditionals 1 and 2*

**THE ECONOMIST**   1   Look at this advertisement for *The Economist* magazine and make sure that you understand the joke.

**"I never read
The Economist."**

Management trainee. Aged 42.

2   Think of ways of completing these sentences.

1   If you buy *The Economist*, ...
2   Unless you buy *The Economist*, ...
3   If you didn't know anything about *The Economist*, this advert ...
4   You won't like *The Economist* if ...
5   If you're studying business, ...
6   If I were a middle-aged failure, ...

**IRN-BRU**   1   Ask and answer three *if* questions about this advert. Think about the advert itself and possible responses to it.

"IRN-BRU KEEPS
ME YOUNG
AND BEAUTIFUL,
UNLIKE
MY DAUGHTER."

2   Think of current adverts that you both know and ask and answer *if* questions about them. Compare your ideas with another pair.

**ADVERTS AND YOU**   Which of the adverts on these pages do you think is the most effective? Explain why.

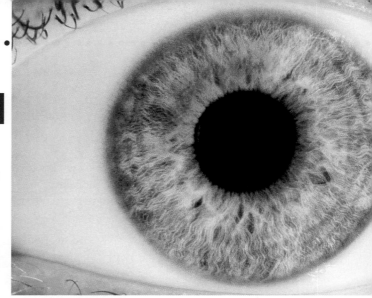

## *Using NLP*

**NLP AND PERSUASION**

Neuro Linguistic Programming (NLP) is a way of explaining how people think and behave. In his book *Who Dares Sells*, Patrick Ellis writes about how NLP can help people to influence others. Read the text and then answer the questions below.

How can NLP help in day to day communication? Some people tend to use expressions like 'I see what you mean' or 'It looks to me' – in other words, they use phrases that make reference to some kind of imagery or visual activity. Others use words like 'I feel I am coming to grips with the situation', suggesting that they relate to the world according to the sense of feeling. Yet others use words like 'tune into' or 'I hear you', suggesting thinking based on the sense of sound. One can hear in people's language which sensory system they are using for thinking at any moment in time.

The information can be of great value to the salesperson when trying to establish the buyer's needs and wants. For example, in a car showroom, the buyer might say, 'I want a good, solid, comfortable car' (suggesting they are thinking about its feel). In this selling situation, if the salesperson responds by saying, 'Well, let me show you this one' or 'Look at these features,' the seller is not responding to the way the buyer is thinking about the car.

1 Why does Patrick Ellis say that the salesperson in his example is not responding to the way that the buyer is thinking about the car?

2 Which of these phrases do you think the salesperson should use in reply? Explain why.

*It sounds as if this car would be right for you.*

*I'll talk you through the whole range.*

**Let's focus on your real needs.**

I think you would feel comfortable with this model.

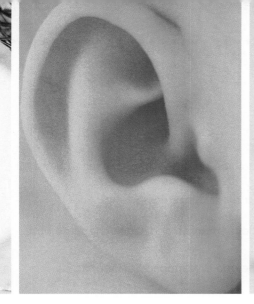

**SIGHT, SOUND OR FEELING**

**1** Look at the box and find two sentences with similar meanings to each of the following.
▪ We don't agree. ▪ It's true. ▪ I understand. ▪ Goodbye.

*I get the picture.* **I'll be in touch.** Hope to hear from you.

I'm not sure we see eye to eye. *It's beyond a shadow of a doubt.* **It's as solid as a rock.** I've got a handle on it.

**I don't think we're on the same wavelength.**

**2** Match each of the sentences in the box to one of the senses of sight, sound and feeling.

**ON THE DOORSTEP**

**1** In both dialogues on the recording, a salesperson is calling at someone's house to try to sell them some new windows. As you listen, decide which of these three senses relates to each person.

| | SIGHT | SOUND | FEELING |
|---|---|---|---|
| Salesman | | | |
| Mrs Knight | | | |
| Saleswoman | | | |
| Mr Morrison | | | |

**2** Listen to the dialogues again and write down as many phrases related to sight, sound and feeling as possible.

Compare your lists with others in the class.

**NLP AND YOU**

Talk about these questions.

*1* Can you think of similar examples of the use of sight, sound and feeling in your own language(s)? Explain – in English!

*2* Which of the senses of sight, sound and feeling do you normally use in your speech? Do others in the group agree with your opinion?

*3* To what extent do you think that the ideas of NLP are helpful in persuading and influencing others?

# doing **business 1** *Selling*

**BUYING A CAR**    In this article, the American writer Stanley Bing talks about his experience of trying to buy a car.

**1** 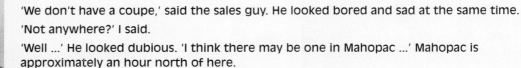 Read the article and make a list of things that the salesman does wrong.

> 'We don't have a coupe,' said the sales guy. He looked bored and sad at the same time.
>
> 'Not anywhere?' I said.
>
> 'Well ...' He looked dubious. 'I think there may be one in Mahopac ...' Mahopac is approximately an hour north of here.
>
> I wondered if I was missing something.
>
> 'So you bring it down here and I'll test drive it,' I offered. 'If I like it, I'll buy it.'
>
> 'We can't bring it down here unless you've already bought it,' he said.
>
> 'You want me to buy a car I've never seen or, like, touched?'
>
> I wasn't quite getting this. Didn't they want me to buy a car?
>
> An uncomfortable silence ensued.
>
> I asked him if he would call me if one sort of accidentally came in or something.
>
> He said he would. I guess one never came in, because he never called.
>
> *Fortune 8.11.99*

**GLOSSARY**

coupe    *a two-door car with a sloping back*

ensued    *followed*

**2** Listen to the way that the same situation is handled on the recording. In what ways does the saleswoman handle the situation better?

**3** How typical is Stanley Bing's experience? How did salespeople treat you the last time you tried to buy an expensive item?

**OVERCOMING OBJECTIONS**    One of the most difficult things to do in any kind of selling is to overcome objections that your potential customer might have. Talk about what you would say in the following three situations. After each one, compare your ideas with the dialogues on the recording.

**Situation 1**

You are selling an expensive computer system to the directors of a small firm. Look at the picture to see what they say when you've explained the benefits of the system that you're offering. How do you respond?

Listen to the way that the saleswoman on the recording copes with the situation.

*1* What does she suggest? Is it very different from your idea?

*2* What are the good points about the way she copes with this situation?

This is a big decision and we need some time to think about it.

I'm sorry, I really can't make up my mind.

**Situation 2**

Your dog has just had puppies and you are trying to sell one of them to a family that lives near you. Look at the picture to see what the woman from the family says after playing with the puppies for half an hour. What's the best way to persuade her to buy one of the puppies?

Listen to what the man says and talk about these questions.

1 In which situations wouldn't you use the man's tactic?
2 Which other situations would this tactic work in? Think of at least two.

**Situation 3**

You are trying to sell a new TV to a married couple. You can tell that they like what you're offering, but look at what the man says at the end of your conversation. What do you say next?

No, I'm afraid it's too expensive.

Listen to what the salesman says next and talk about these questions.

1 What is the good point about the way that the salesman handles the situation?
2 What compromise does he have to make by using this tactic?

**SALES ROLES**  Role play these situations, using the ideas on these pages when appropriate. In each case, the salesperson should prepare by thinking of three features that make their product attractive.

❙ **A** You are a telephone salesperson. It's your job to call a number of people at home and try to persuade them to change to a new credit card. It offers all the usual credit card services but has a rate of interest that's 0.5% lower than any other card currently on the market.

**B** You are sitting at home when the salesperson from the credit card company rings. You're not particularly interested in changing your credit card but you're prepared to listen.

❙ **B** You are a salesperson in a car showroom. It's late on Friday afternoon and you need to sell one more car to meet your target for the week.

**A** You stroll into a car showroom to look around. You're not particularly interested in buying a new car at the moment – unless, of course, someone makes you an offer you can't refuse!

# doing business 2 *Taking an order*

**ASSESSING A SALESMAN**

Listen to this salesman as he tries to take a customer's order. What are the good points and the bad points about the way he does this? Make a list and then compare yours with other pairs in the class.

**McCORMACK'S ADVICE**

Mark McCormack is the world's leading sports agent and an expert in business communication. He gives this advice to salespeople in his book *What they don't Teach you at Harvard Business School.*

Read the text and answer these questions.

1 Why does Mark McCormack say that it is a bad idea to praise your customers' decision to buy?
2 What does he mean by crossing every 't' and dotting every 'i'? Why does he think that this is a bad idea?
3 What do you think he would say about the performance of the salesman in the scene you just heard?
4 Do you agree with Mark McCormack? In which situations do you think his advice would *not* work?

*Mark McCormack*

I can't tell you how many times I've seen this happen: a sale is made and the salesman immediately raises suspicion by heaping hyperbolic praise on the buyer's judgment: 'You won't regret this.' 'The best deal you've ever made.' Even the most trusting person will start to wonder, 'What have I just committed myself to?'

Once you've made the sale, anything else you say about it can only work against you. So, change the subject. Talk about the buyer's golf game, his kids – anything but how extraordinarily brilliant he is for buying your product.

Even worse than the flatterers are the salesmen who insist right then and there, on crossing every 't' and dotting every 'i' – 'Great. Now let's go over these points again to make sure we are in total agreement.' At best, this approach dampens enthusiasm. At worst, whole deals can become unravelled.

**‖ GLOSSARY ‖**

hyperbolic *excessive*
flatterers *people who give other people too much praise*
unravelled *undone*

**SALES SITUATIONS**

Discuss what you think it's best to do in these situations.

■ You have just shaken hands on an agreement with an important customer, when your customer's boss knocks on the door of the meeting room. Your customer's boss hasn't met you before and asks to be introduced. She then says, 'Talk me through this deal you've been discussing.' How do you handle the situation?

■ You are a salesperson for an office-cleaning company. For several weeks, you have been trying to persuade a medium-sized company to start using your services. At the end of your third meeting with the company's facilities manager, he agrees to sign a six-month contract to use your services. However, just after you've reached agreement, he says, 'Before you go, I'd like you to talk me through the contract line by line.' How do you respond?

**SHOOTING FISH**     In the film *Shooting Fish*, we see a salesman called Stephen Wolford making a sales presentation about a new kind of computer to a group of businesspeople. At the end of the presentation, one of the businesspeople, Mr Greenway, says that he's interested in buying some of the machines.

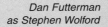 Read how Stephen Wolford handles the situation and talk about these questions.

*1* Why do you think that Wolford acts in this way?
*2* Is it a successful tactic in this situation?
*3* In what other situations do you think it could be effective? When might it not work?

| | |
|---|---|
| GREENWAY | That is remarkable. It is incredible. I'm interested. |
| WOLFORD | Good. Good. Oh, God. Look, we've run over. I'm going to call you in a couple of months. |
| GREENWAY | No, no, no, no, no. I really am interested. |
| WOLFORD | No, no, no. Look, don't get me wrong. I think that that's good. It's just that there's another group coming in and I've got to set up. |
| GREENWAY | We might want eight. |
| WOLFORD | Right. Um ... look, OK, here's the thing. This next company, if this works out, they're going to want this month's entire delivery. |
| GREENWAY | Twelve, we want twelve. Now. |
| WOLFORD | You're going to hate me for this. OK, look, here's the deal. If you can give me a 10% deposit now, I think I can hold them for you. |
| GREENWAY | Skivvings, the cheque book. It's a pleasure doing business with you, Mr Wolford. |

*Dan Futterman
as Stephen Wolford*

█ **GLOSSARY** █

we've run over    *we've taken too much time*
another group    *another group of possible customers*
Skivvings    *the name of Greenway's colleague*

**SALES ROLES**     Role play these situations.

▮ **A** You're a salesperson for a company that makes music systems. If you sell five more new systems by the end of today, you will hit your sales target and receive a large bonus payment.
   **B** You run a medium-sized electrical goods shop and you would like to buy **A**'s new music systems. However, you feel you only have room for three of them in your shop.

▮ **A** You own a courier company which has a small fleet of identical vans. For the past ten years you have always bought the same kind of van because they have been reliable and because people associate them with your company. Now you have decided to buy two more of them.
   **B** You are a salesperson for a company that sells vans. You know that the company has stopped producing them and there are only twelve of this kind of van left.

# issues
## *Marketing tales*

**ORDINARY POWDER**

**1** Listen to a report about an unusual marketing strategy from Siberia and answer these questions.

*1* How was Ariel advertising its washing powder at that time?

*2* What idea did this give the Russians in Angarsk?

*3* What were the advantages of the Russian approach?

**2** Now discuss these questions.

*1* What is the disadvantage of their approach?

*2* Would the Siberian strategy work in your country? Why – or why not?

**PERCEPTION AND THE MERMAID**

Read this text and the text opposite and discuss the questions that follow.

## Subliminal perception

In 1957, an American marketing man called James Vicary announced the results of an experiment that he had conducted at a cinema in New Jersey. Over a period of six weeks he claimed that he had used a machine called a tachistoscope to flash messages lasting no more than 1/3000th of a second onto the screen while audiences were watching a movie. The messages said simply 'Drink Coke' and 'Buy popcorn'. Although the messages were too quick for the audience to realise that they were seeing them, the results they produced were astounding. Sales of Coke at the cinema increased by nearly 58% and sales of popcorn rose by nearly 18%.

Scientists, however, were not convinced, and Vicary was later forced to admit that his 'experiment' had been a hoax staged in an attempt to revive his failing business.

But although Vicary had been discredited, the memory of his experiment has still not faded. For example, it is known that the US military has used techniques of subliminal perception to train fighter pilots to recognise enemy planes. And there have often been claims that the music played in supermarkets and department stores contains subliminal messages such as 'Buy more' or 'Do not steal'. The companies involved have usually – although not always – denied the claims.

The problem is: if subliminal marketing techniques are being used, how would we know about it?

**GLOSSARY**

hoax *trick*

*1* What is subliminal perception? Explain in your own words.

*2* Do you believe that subliminal marketing techniques are in use today? Do you know of any evidence – or any rumours – that could support your opinion?

*3* Do you think that there are other ways that marketing tries to influence people subconsciously? Give examples.

# Barnum and the mermaid

One of the most brilliant marketing men in history was the American showman, Phineas T. Barnum. Barnum delighted the American public with shows full of clever tricks, and amazed them with the extraordinary objects that he found for his museum in New York.

One day in 1842, Barnum bought a very strange skeleton. It had the head of a monkey and the body of a fish. He was told that it was the skeleton of a mermaid. Of course, he didn't believe it and after some research, he discovered that the mermaid's skeleton was a hoax and had actually been made in Japan.

But Barnum wasn't worried. He persuaded newspapers around the country to publish stories that a mermaid had been captured in Fiji. He also sent them paintings of mermaids that they could use as illustrations. Before long, people right across America were discussing whether mermaids really existed.

When Barnum put his mermaid's skeleton on display in his museum, excited crowds poured through the doors to see the extraordinary object for themselves. No wonder Barnum's most famous saying was: 'There's a sucker born every minute.'

## ▌ GLOSSARY ▌

sucker    *a person who is easily deceived or tricked*

1  Can you think of any modern examples of a similar marketing strategy? Describe how they worked.
2  Do you think there is anything wrong with this kind of marketing campaign? Explain your reasons.
3  Do you agree with Barnum that 'There's a sucker born every minute'?

## BARNUM AND YOU

**1** Choose one of the ideas below and think about how you could use a strategy like Barnum's to get people interested. Think about how you would use one or more of these media:

newspapers and magazines        TV and radio        the Internet

▌ a new soft drink that contains a special ingredient that is supposed to give people lots of energy (although it hasn't been proved scientifically)
▌ an album by a new rock band who are supposed to be the greatest thing since Nirvana (although their lead singer is in his early fifties and looks like a bank manager)
▌ a modern art exhibition in which all the pictures are plain white sheets of paper or canvas

**2** Make up another idea and ask another group to work out a marketing strategy for it.

# 7 paranoia

When I close the
fridge door, does the
light really go off?

**paranoia** an unreasonable fear that something bad is about to happen

Longman Business English Dictionary

**FEELINGS ABOUT
THE FUTURE**

Which of these words best describes your feelings about the future? Explain why.

*paranoia* *confidence* excitement **hope** *anxiety* panic

**ONLY THE PARANOID
SURVIVE**

Andy Groves is the CEO of Intel Corporation, the world's largest producer of computer chips. The title of his most famous book is *Only the Paranoid Survive*.

Read this story about a serious crisis in Intel's recent history and then talk about the questions below.

Is it progress
if a cannibal
starts to eat
with a knife
and fork?

In 1994, just after Intel had started production of their new Pentium processor, they discovered a very slight fault in one of the chips that was responsible for mathematical calculations. After an extensive study, they found that this error would affect the average spreadsheet user about once in every 27,000 years. Intel decided that it would quietly make the necessary modifications to the chip.

But Intel's specialists were not the only people who had spotted the problem. A maths professor noticed a small error in his new Pentium processor while he was working on an extremely complex calculation. The professor posted his observation on the Internet, where it was reported by a few specialist computer magazines. Before long, the international broadcaster CNN had picked up on the story and it had spread around the world. Major newspapers ran headlines on Intel, Pentium users demanded free replacement chips and the computer giant IBM stopped the delivery of Pentium-based machines.

To regain control of the situation, Intel agreed to the free replacement of hundreds of thousands of Pentium processors. The tiny error in the processor eventually cost the company over $475 million.

*1* In Andy Groves' situation, would you have told the public about the Pentium error when it was first discovered?

*2* Do you think that the media were right to give so much publicity to the problem?

*3* Does the story explain why Groves believes that only the paranoid survive?

## THE SHOSHONE GRAVEYARD

Read this story about a strange problem faced by Steven Spielberg and answer the questions below.

In 1996, Steven Spielberg was faced with a real-life situation that sounded like it came from the plot of one of his more bizarre movies. Spielberg's company DreamWorks was planning a major property development on an area of marshy land just to the north of Los Angeles International Airport.

But before any work could start, DreamWorks learnt of a rather unusual problem. Chief Vera Rocha, leader of the Shoshone Gabrilieno native Americans, claimed that the area was sacred to his people. It contained an ancient Shoshone cemetery and was cursed for the white man. It would, he said, be a graveyard of their dreams.

1  How do you think a paranoid survivor would handle this situation?
2  In Steven Spielberg's position, how would you have handled it?

How do I know that I'm not the star of someone else's soap opera?

## THE COMMONWEALTH SENTINEL

This story is about forgetting things. Read it and then answer the questions below.

In 1965, the entrepreneur Lionel Burleigh came up with a great business idea. He decided to launch a newspaper called the *Commonwealth Sentinel* that would be aimed at the many people in London who came from British Commonwealth countries. He worked day and night organising the newspaper's contents and selling advertising space and looked forward to the day when he would be a wealthy man.

However, on the morning of the first issue, he woke up to find 50,000 copies of his newspaper on the street outside his hotel. Burleigh had been so busy sorting out the details of his newspaper's launch that he'd forgotten to organise any distribution!

Nobody heard of the *Commonwealth Sentinel* again.

1  In your business life, do you ever get the feeling that you've forgotten something important? If so, give an example.
2  Have you ever really forgotten something crucial to your business or your career? Tell the story.

## PARANOIA AND YOU

Discuss the following questions.

1  Do you agree that in business life only the paranoid survive?
2  Are there times when paranoia has made you take the wrong decisions? Explain.

Why do cats always stare at me?

# GRAMMAR REVIEW

**FIVE FUTURES**

Look at the sentences on the left and match them with the descriptions on the right. Notice the future form used in each case.

| | |
|---|---|
| I'll send the fax immediately. | an intention |
| I think it's going to rain later. | a fixed plan |
| I'm flying to Rio de Janeiro next Monday. | a promise |
| The meeting starts at ten to nine. | a short-term prediction |
| I'm going to sort out these files. | an official timetable |

▌ *For more on these points, turn to page 131.* ▌

**A MANAGER'S NIGHTMARE**

1  Listen to a manager's nightmare on the recording and answer these questions.

*1* What will the manager be doing at three o'clock tomorrow?

*2* What does he think won't have happened by that time?

*3* Why is he so worried about the competition?

*4* What does he think he'll be doing next year?

2 Which of your answers to the questions above talk about something that will or won't be in progress in the future? Which talk about something that will or won't have been completed in the future?

3  Listen to the nightmare again and do the following.

*1* Write down as many things as possible in these two categories:

▌ things that will or will not be in progress in the future
▌ things that will have been or won't have been completed in the future

*2* Compare your lists with others in the group.

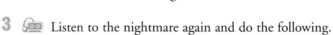

**CHECK**

To talk about something that will be in progress at a future time, use the **future continuous**.

*By this time next year, we'll be selling our products into Asia.*

To talk about something that will be completed by a future time, use the **future perfect**.

*By next June, we'll have restructured the whole department.*

▌ *For more on these points, turn to page 132.* ▌

# Future forms

**THE BT TECHNOLOGY CALENDAR**

This is a technology calendar of predictions made by Ian Pearson of British Telecom Labs. Some of the predictions may sound fantastic but they are all based on current projects at research laboratories around the world.

| | EARLIEST | EXPECTED | LATEST |
|---|---|---|---|
| Artificial human brain cells | 2012 | 2017 | 2022 |
| 3D TV without special glasses | 2008 | 2012 | 2016 |
| Deep underground cities in Japan | 2015 | 2020 | 2025 |
| Extension of average lifespan to over 100 | 2015 | 2020 | 2025 |
| Human knowledge exceeded by machine knowledge | 2012 | 2017 | 2022 |
| Smart skin for intelligent clothing and direct human repair | 2015 | 2020 | 2025 |
| Thought recognition used for computer input | 2020 | 2025 | 2030 |
| Robots for guiding blind people | 2010 | 2015 | 2020 |
| Near Earth space tours | 2010 | 2015 | 2020 |
| Direct brain link between humans and computers | 2025 | 2030 | 2035 |

**1** Write sentences about each of Ian Pearson's predictions, using either the future continuous or future perfect tense.

*1* By 2022, scientists ... (develop)
*2* By 2016, viewers ... (watch)
*3* By 2025, in Japan, engineers ... (build)
*4* By 2025, most people ... (live)
*5* By 2022, machine knowledge ... (exceed)
*6* By 2025, doctors ... (use)
*7* By 2030, computers ... (use)
*8* By 2020, robots ... (guide)
*9* By 2020, holidaymakers ... (take)
*10* By 2035, scientists ... (introduce)

**2** Rank the predictions from the most probable (1) to the least probable (10). Compare your rankings with the rest of the class and explain why you have ranked the predictions in this way.

**YOUR PREDICTIONS** Think about the future and do the following.

*1* Make a list of at least five things which you hope to have achieved by this time next year.
*2* Think of five activities that you expect to be doing this time next year.
*3* Make five predictions about the way in which technology will change our lives over the next thirty years.

## *Business imagery*

**A SHOCK TO THE SYSTEM**

At the start of the film *A Shock to the System*, an advertising executive called Graham Marshall (Michael Caine) meets his boss George Brewster (John McMartin) on the way to their office in New York.

 Read the script and answer these questions.

1 What mood does George seem to be in?
2 What does George think is happening to their company?
3 What does George think will happen to him?

GRAHAM  You look fit today, George, ready to do battle?

GEORGE  It's all up for me and I've done what I can for you. Now let's just read our papers.

GRAHAM  I think you're jumping the gun.

GEORGE  Oh, come on, the whole point of these takeovers is to sell off the assets and put old fools like me out to pasture. I can hear the fat lady singing, Graham. I can hear her singing ... Let's face it, Graham, the new people, it's all gadgets and the bottom line.

GRAHAM  I hear you George.

GEORGE  Stop them early or they'll run right over you.

**IMAGES**

Think about the images used in the script above and fill the gaps in this table.

| IMAGE | WHERE IS IT FROM? | WHAT DOES IT MEAN HERE? |
| --- | --- | --- |
| to do battle | war | |
| | athletics | |
| to put someone out to pasture | | to end a person's career |
| to hear the fat lady singing | | it's the end |
| the bottom line | accountancy | |
| | driving | |

**SOURCES OF IMAGERY**    Research has shown that these are four of the most common sources of images in business English.

| SPORT AND GAMES | ANIMALS AND THE NATURAL WORLD |
|---|---|
| *The global economy is like a corporate Olympics.* | *Workers have been treated like dog food for the past 150 years.* |
| Rosabeth Moss Kanter, business guru | Tom Peters, business guru |

| WAR | A JOURNEY |
|---|---|
| *Business is war.* | *We're on a pirate ship at sea.* |
| Japanese saying | Ted Turner, boss of CNN |

**1** Look back at the film script. Which of the images used there fit into these four categories?

**2** Underline the ten images used in the sentences below. Which of the four areas do they come from? Can you work out what they mean?

1  I've decided to get out of the rat race and buy a little farm in the country.
2  This company has left its past behind. We are now sailing into uncharted waters.
3  What this industry needs more than anything is a level playing field.
4  We know that the current boom won't last forever, but the government believes that the economy will have a soft landing.
5  In the software industry today, it's a dog-eat-dog situation.
6  There's a rumour that a corporate raider has started buying shares in our company.
7  Our last advertising campaign was a bit of an own goal. I think our competitors benefited from it more than we did.
8  This new marketing strategy is going to blow the competition out of the water.
9  She knew that the project was going to lose a lot of money, so she jumped ship before anyone found out.
10  Of course I can't tell you exactly how many units we'll sell, but I'll give you a ballpark figure of around 15,000 in the first year.

**IMAGES AND YOU**    Talk about the following.

1  Think of other words or phrases that use images based on the four themes above, e.g. *sales target, corporate jungle.* What do they mean?
2  Think of a simple image that describes business life or an aspect of it. Explain it to the others in the group.

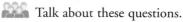 **doing business 1** *Keeping customers*

**DO YOU COMPLAIN?**

 Talk about these questions.

*1* When was the last time you complained about a product or service? What did you do?

*2* When was the last time that you were dissatisfied with something but didn't complain about it? Why didn't you complain?

**COMPLAINTS PLEASE!**

In this newspaper article, the journalist Hamish McRae explains why complaints can be a good thing for a business.

Read the article and then answer these questions.

*1* According to McRae, in what way is a complaint a gift from a customer to a company? Do you agree?

*2* Why is it more important to keep existing customers than to win new ones?

*3* What advice on handling complaints positively does he give? What advice would you add to the list?

# You must worry if your customers don't complain

HAMISH MCRAE

A customer complains if he or she has or wants to have a continuing relationship with the company (that provides the service or supplies the goods). Not to complain if there is something wrong means the customer does not give a hoot whether the business succeeds or fails.

This principle – that a complaint is a gift that a customer gives a business to help it perform better – applies to manufacturing and service industries.

The practical starting point is that it is not only much easier to increase sales to existing customers than it is to win new ones, but existing customers are more valuable. It costs about five times as much to win a new customer as it does to keep an existing one. But cost aside, replacing 1,000 existing customers with 1,000 new ones might seem a straight trade. It is not, because the lost customers give the company a bad reputation and make it harder to bring in the new ones.

In the US, a person who is pleased with the purchase of their car tells on average eight people about it; a customer who is unhappy with the purchase tells 22 people. Some of those 22 will tell others, and so on.

How do you use complaints positively? The answer quite simply is common sense presented in an orderly way: be polite, listen, welcome the complaint, try to make sure the customer leaves feeling satisfied.

**■ GLOSSARY ■**

not to give a hoot  *not to care at all*

The Independent Business Review *12.5.99*

**HANDLING COMPLAINTS**

The British TV comedy *Fawlty Towers* is set in a chaotic hotel on the south coast of England. In this scene, a couple are complaining to the hotel's owner, Basil Fawlty, about the food.

**1** What mistakes do you think Basil makes in the way that he handles the complaint? Compare your ideas with others in the class.

**2** Role play the same situation (a person complaining about the food in a restaurant) and this time make sure that the customer is happy at the end of the conversation.

| | |
|---|---|
| MR JOHNSTONE | Er ... my wife ... |
| BASIL | Yes? |
| MRS JOHNSTONE | I think those prawns might be a bit off. |
| BASIL | Oh, I don't think so. |
| MRS JOHNSTONE | Well, they do taste rather funny. |
| BASIL | Well, no one else has complained. |
| MRS JOHNSTONE | Well, I really do think they're off. |
| BASIL | But you've eaten half of them. |
| MRS JOHNSTONE | Well, I didn't notice at the start. |
| BASIL | You didn't notice at the start? |
| MRS JOHNSTONE | Well, it was the sauce, you see. I wasn't sure. |
| BASIL | So you ate half to make sure. |
| MR JOHNSTONE | Look, my wife thinks they're off. |
| BASIL | Well, what am I supposed to do about it ... do you want another first course? |
| MRS JOHNSTONE | No, thank you. |
| MR JOHNSTONE | You're sure? |
| MRS JOHNSTONE | No, really, I'll just have the main. |
| MR JOHNSTONE | Well, we'll just cancel it. |
| BASIL | Cancel it? Oh, deduct it from the bill, is that what you mean? |
| MR JOHNSTONE | Well, as it's inedible ... |
| BASIL | Well, only half of it's inedible, apparently. |
| MR JOHNSTONE | Well, deduct half now and if my wife brings the other half up during the night, we'll claim the balance in the morning. |

**❙ GLOSSARY ❙**

to be off   *to be no longer good to eat*

**COMPLAINING ROLES**

Role play these situations.

**❙ A** You are complaining about your transatlantic flight, which has been delayed by four hours.
  **B** You are a representative of the airline, which is the victim of an air traffic controllers' dispute.

**❙ B** You are phoning to complain about the failure of a new software program.
  **A** You are a member of the software company's helpline team.

**❙ A** You are complaining about your hotel room because it's a hot summer night and loud music from a bar opposite is keeping you awake.
  **B** You are the hotel manager and your hotel is completely full.

**❙ A** You are complaining about the fact that your office photocopier has broken down for the third time in a week.
  **B** You are a salesperson from the photocopier company who wants to sell **A** a new model.

# doing business 2 *Body language*

**7-38-55**    On the basis of his research while he was a professor of psychology at the University of Los Angeles, Albert Mehrabian developed this formula to describe how communication works.

> 7% of the meaning of a message is contained in the words that you actually say.
> 38% of the meaning is communicated by your tone of voice.
> 55% of the meaning comes from visual cues like posture, gesture and expression.

From your experience, would you agree with Professor Mehrabian's formula? Explain why – or why not.

**THE PROFESSIONAL MAN**    In his book about Silicon Valley, *The New New Thing*, this is how Michael Lewis describes one of the computer industry's leading business figures.

> HE HAD MASTERED the unnaturally sincere tone of voice of the Professional Man. When he wished to indicate seriousness, he dropped his chin down to his throat. When he took you aside to have a word, he looked and sounded as if he was giving a speech to an audience of a thousand people. To stress his points, which were rarely pointed or stressful, he'd press his thumb against his forefinger as if he had just caught a fly by the wing. He wore suits. He hated strife. He loved consensus, or at any rate the idea of it.

When you've read the text, do the following.

*1* Take turns to say this sentence in the style of the businessman described. Try to copy both his body language and his tone of voice.

You must understand that we may experience some difficulty in achieving all of this year's financial objectives.

*2* How many of the businessman's mannerisms did you spot in your partner's performance?
*3* Do you know anyone who acts in a similar way? Are you impressed by this kind of 'Professional Man'? Explain why – or why not.
*4* If a businesswoman was trying to be a 'Professional Woman', how do you think that her body language might be different?

**READING BODY
LANGUAGE**

**1** How would you interpret the gestures shown in these cartoons?

1 Hand over the mouth while speaking

2 Standing with hands on hips

3 Head tilted to the side

4 Chin supported by fingers

5 Arms folded

6 Steepled fingers

7 Picking fluff from clothing

8 Scratching the neck

**2** Turn to page 126 to find out how these gestures would probably be interpreted in British/American business culture. Are any of the interpretations surprising to you?

**BODY LANGUAGE
AND YOU**

Talk about these questions.

*1* How important do you think that body language is in business? Explain.
*2* What advice can you give to others in the group about appropriate body language in business?

# issues

## *Is Big Brother watching you?*

**BIG BROTHER**

Big Brother was the name of the head of state in George Orwell's novel *Nineteen Eighty-Four*. Although nobody ever saw him in person, there were pictures of him everywhere, accompanied by the message 'Big Brother is watching you'. When George Orwell wrote his novel, Big Brother was clearly a political figure, but in the modern world, could he be someone from big business?

**BIG BROTHER TODAY**

According to the American Management Association, nearly two thirds of large American companies electronically monitor their staff. This illustration shows the legal position regarding the relationship between employer and employee in the USA.

 Look at the text and talk about these questions.

1 Do any of the company's rights surprise you? Why – or why not?
2 How different is the situation for employees in your country?

**YOUR KNOWLEDGE**
Workers can be sent to jail for disclosing their company's intellectual property secrets. Employers can also claim the right to innovations made by workers even if they are made outside work.

**YOUR MESSAGES**
Employers can listen to phone calls and messages for any reasonable business purpose, without telling the employee.

**YOUR PERSONAL SPACE**
Some companies have started installing video cameras in work spaces to monitor performance. So far, lavatories, showers and changing rooms have not been targeted.

**YOUR BODY**
Employers have the right to do random drugs tests on employees. Many also insist on genetic tests in order to minimise their healthcare costs.

**YOUR COMPUTER**
Employers can search all files stored on an office PC. They can also read all e-mail stored on a hard disk or server.

**YOUR DOCUMENTS**
Desk drawers and filing cabinets belong to the company and it has the right to search them at any time.

**YOU AND YOUR COMPANY**

 Talk about what you would do in these situations.

You are a full time employee of a computer software development company. While you are on holiday with your family, you have a great idea for a new application. What is the right thing to do – develop your idea in your own time or give your idea to your company?

When you join your company, the personnel officer explains that there is a strict no-smoking policy and that all employees must sign a document to say that they do not smoke. Although you are normally a non-smoker, after a private dinner late one night you decide to have a cigarette. The following morning at work, the company asks you to report to the medical officer for a random blood test. What do you do?

**BIG BROTHER TOMORROW**

Read this article about the possible future of employer–employee relations and then talk about these questions.

1 How would this technology benefit employers?
2 How would it benefit employees?
3 Under what circumstances would you accept a microchip implant?

## COMPANIES SEEK CHIP IMPLANTS TO CONTROL STAFF

**Big Brother could soon be watching from the inside. Several international companies are consulting scientists on ways of developing microchip implants for their workers to measure their timekeeping and whereabouts.**

The microchip would be surgically implanted in workers' forearms and would enable firms to track staff all around a building. The data could enable them to draw up estimates of workers' efficiency and productivity.

The system could also be of benefit by being programmed to switch on lights, computers and heating systems as workers entered a room – and turn them off when they left.

*Sunday Times 9.5.99*

**BIG BROTHER AND YOU**

 Talk about these questions.

1 What signs of Big Brother have you noticed in your workplace?
2 What signs of Big Brother have you seen in society in general?
3 Do you think that any of these changes will have a good or bad effect on your life?

# 8 the **deal**

**THE ART OF THE DEAL**     In his story *False Accounting*, the Somali writer Nuruddin Farah writes about negotiating in Africa. Read the text and then talk about the questions below.

> **B**argaining is an art form is some cultures. For me the process becomes not only a bid to alter the asking price to my advantage, but also a means of making personal contact. The man who comes to our house once a week with neatly-wrapped vegetables on the saddle of his bicycle insists that I listen to his stories in exchange for any discount that he might give.
>
> Time is not money in Africa, where words are accorded a higher value than in Europe. In my day, I have known salesmen to be put out by a buyer who has the money to pay for the item in question but not the words with which to grease the gears of human communication.

**▌ GLOSSARY ▌**

to be accorded   *to be given*
to be put out   *to be offended*
to grease the gears   *to help the process*

1   For you, is business about making personal contact or is it about making money?
2   What is the value of words in a business deal?
3   Do you feel that time is money? Explain.
4   In what ways is your attitude to negotiating different to Nuruddin Farah's?

## THREE CULTURES

Read what three European books say about negotiating in three different cultures – Japan, the Arab world and the USA – and do 1–4 below.

**M**OST regard bargaining as natural entertainment and many have honed their techniques to a fine degree. For many, bargaining is business: no other business activity is more important or more stimulating. Some people can be overwhelmed by the sudden and often powerful theatrical styles involved, especially coming from someone who was apparently an example of politeness and hospitality.

Don't they Know it's Friday?
*by Jeremy Williams*

To do business, you must make some effort to understand how they function. If you are in a hurry, or do not consider personal relationships of any value, or cannot abide highly polite exchanges of conversation, gifts and kindnesses, you are unlikely to secure much interest in what you have come to sell (or buy).

Everything is Negotiable
*by Gavin Kennedy*

The Seven Cultures of
Capitalism *by Trompenaars and
Hampden-Turner*

They like to get to the point. 'What's your proposition? Can we do business? I'll send you a fax with the terms of the suggested contract.' No one wants to 'beat about the bush' because 'time is money'. After all, the world is full of people with whom it might be nice to drink tea, but not full of potential business partners. So, 'Let's get down to basics. What have you got?'

### ▍ GLOSSARY ▍

to hone   *to practise, refine*
to beat about the bush   *to spend a long time getting to the point*
cannot abide   *have no patience with*

*1* Guess which culture is described by each text. Give reasons for your decisions.
*2* Check your answers on page 126. To what extent do you think that these descriptions are accurate?
*3* Using your own knowledge of these cultures, what information or opinions would you add to or subtract from each text?
*4* What advice would you give to a foreign businessperson planning to negotiate in your country for the first time?

## THE DEAL AND YOU

Read these three situations and then talk about these questions.

*1* In which of the situations would you attempt to negotiate? Explain why – or why not.
*2* If you decided to negotiate, how would you begin the negotiation in each situation?

You visit a clothes shop during the sale period and see a beautiful jacket with a 25% reduction. You return a few days later to discover that the shop's sale has ended and that the jacket is once more on sale at the full price. Do you try to negotiate with the sales assistant?

During your lunch hour, you visit an antiques market where you see an antique chair that you'd like to buy. However, the stall's owner has left his teenage daughter in charge of the stall while he goes out to lunch. Do you attempt to bargain with her to get a better price?

You want to buy a new car. You go into your local car dealership, where the prices of all cars are clearly stated. However, you have seen cheaper prices for the same cars on the Internet. Do you attempt to get a better deal from the car dealership?

# GRAMMAR REVIEW

**THE HAGGLER'S HANDBOOK**

In their book about negotiating (or 'haggling'), Leonard Koren and Peter Goodman offer some advice on the subject.

Read the text and talk about these questions.

*1* When someone says 'no' in a negotiation, how should you interpret it?
*2* If you find something that you can't agree about, what should you do?
*3* In your experience, is the writers' advice good?

Don't be <u>put off</u> by the word 'no'. The word 'no' in a negotiation is usually code for 'not right now' or 'not exactly' or 'maybe, but I'm not going to <u>give in</u> just now'. Take phrases like 'impossible', 'never', 'no way' as invitations to <u>keep on</u> talking. After all, if the other person really thought that a deal was out of the question, he would <u>get up</u> and <u>walk out</u>.

<u>Skip over</u> the points that are <u>bogging</u> you <u>down</u> and <u>come back</u> to them later. Rather than jeopardise the entire negotiation, suggest that the sticking point be <u>put aside</u> for now and returned to after other matters have been <u>sorted out</u>.

*The Haggler's Handbook by Leonard Koren and Peter Goodman*

**MATCH THE MEANINGS**

The underlined words in the text are all phrasal verbs (verb + adverb or preposition). Match each phrasal verb to a verb in the box with a similar meaning.

> **settle** concede **jump** return
> frustrate continue deter
> temporarily forget **leave** stand

> ### CHECK
>
> Remember that some **phrasal verbs** are separable; in other words, it is possible to put the object of the sentence between the verb and the preposition or adverb.
>
> *Don't let it **put** you **off**. Have you **sorted** it out?*
>
> In other cases, they are inseparable – the object needs to come after the preposition or adverb.
>
> *Let's **skip over** it. Don't **give in** now.*
>
> ■ *For more on phrasal verbs, turn to page 141.* ■

# *Phrasal verbs*

**FIVE FAVOURITE PHRASALS**

According to the *Longman Grammar of Spoken and Written English*, the five verbs most often used to form phrasal verbs are: *take, get, come, put, go*. On the left are some of the words that these verbs most frequently go together with.

**1** Choose a combination of verb and adjective/adverb to replace each of the verbs in brackets. When an object (e.g. *it*) is inside the brackets, put that word between the verb and the preposition or adverb (e.g. *pick **it** up*). If necessary, use a dictionary to help you.

*1* After a slow start, sales really (improved) _____ .
*2* Our competitor copied our product by (disassembling it) _____ .
*3* If you're not satisfied with your purchase, (return it) _____ to the shop.
*4* Our company was (bought) _____ by a large American multinational last year.

*1* I (found) _____ a very interesting article about your company in yesterday's newspaper.
*2* How did that (happen) _____ ?
*3* I didn't believe a word he said and later it (emerged) _____ that he was lying.
*4* Sarah left the company last year, but she (returned) _____ to become marketing director last week.

*1* You did well at that meeting. You (proposed) _____ a couple of very good ideas.
*2* You (communicated your point) _____ very clearly.
*3* Hang on just a moment and I'll (connect you) _____ .
*4* I was furious with him. He (humiliated me) _____ in front of everybody in the office.

**2** Choose a combination of verb and adjective/adverb to complete these sentences.

*1* I didn't know you were coming to the office today. When did you _____ from your trip?
*2* It's much harder to do a deal with people if you don't _____ with them.
*3* I'm sorry I'm late. The boss started talking to me and I couldn't _____ from her.
*4* I tried to call you yesterday, but there was a problem with the line and I couldn't _____ .

*1* I'm sorry you can't speak to him. He _____ for lunch about ten minutes ago.
*2* I think there must be a power cut. All the lights _____ about five minutes ago.
*3* I didn't think anyone would like my proposal, but it _____ without any problems.
*4* I don't know why we have to talk about this again. We _____ it in great detail at the last meeting.

**take**
+
apart, back, down, in, off, on, out, over, up

**come**
+
about, across, along, around, back, down, in, off, on, out, over, up

**put**
+
across, away, back, down, forward, in, off, on, out, over, through, up

**get**
+
along, around, away, back, down, in, off, on, out, through, up

**go**
+
about, along, down, in, off, on, out, over, through, up

## *Talking tough*

**BUSINESS STYLE**

This is an e-mail sent by the boss of the American company Healtheon, in which he compares doing business in New York with doing business in other parts of the world.

Read the e-mail and talk about the questions below.

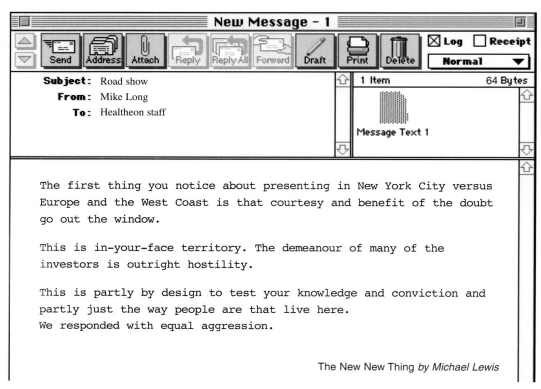

> The first thing you notice about presenting in New York City versus Europe and the West Coast is that courtesy and benefit of the doubt go out the window.
>
> This is in-your-face territory. The demeanour of many of the investors is outright hostility.
>
> This is partly by design to test your knowledge and conviction and partly just the way people are that live here.
> We responded with equal aggression.
>
> *The New New Thing by Michael Lewis*

*1* The writer says that on the West Coast of the USA and in Europe people give you the 'benefit of the doubt', while in New York they are 'in your face'. Which words in the box do you associate with which expression?

| BENEFIT OF THE DOUBT | IN YOUR FACE |
|---|---|
|  |  |
|  |  |
|  |  |

aggression  hostility
courtesy  sympathy
frankness
conviction  modesty

*2* What words can you add to the two lists?

**BUSINESS STYLE AND YOU**

Talk about these questions.

*1* In what ways do you think that it is helpful to have a tough image in business life? In what ways could it be a disadvantage?

*2* In your experience, which business cultures give people 'the benefit of the doubt' and which are 'in your face'?

**THE SAYINGS OF GEKKO**

In the film *Wall Street*, Michael Douglas plays the ruthless, tough-talking New York financier, Gordon Gekko. These are some of his most famous sayings from the movie.

Lunch? You've got to be kidding. Lunch is for wimps.

Christmas is over and business is business.

I loved it at forty, it's an insult at fifty.

Rip their throats out. Stuff them in your garbage compactor.

You'd better get me out or the only job you'll have on this street is sweeping it.

In my book, either you do it right, or you get eliminated.

**▌ GLOSSARY ▌**

to kid   *to joke*

wimp   *a weak person*

garbage compactor   *a machine that squashes rubbish*

Here are some more polite ways of saying the same things. Match each of these sentences to one of Gordon Gekko's sayings.

> If you don't help me, you'll face some very serious consequences.
> You're going to have to be very tough with them.
> We really can't afford any mistakes.
> No, I'm sorry, I'm afraid I can't make lunch today.
> I don't think I can accept it at that price.
> We've got to be realistic about this.

**VIOLENT VERBS**

Businesspeople sometimes like to make their language more colourful by using verbs associated with violent actions.

**1** Find two verbs from the box which you can substitute for each of the verbs that are underlined in these sentences.

grab  annihilate  **rip**  bowl over
tear  knock out  ram
smash  stuff  snatch

*1* <u>Pull</u> their throats out. <u>Put</u> them in your garbage compactor.
*2* When we heard about their special offer, we <u>got</u> as many units as we could.
*3* I was really <u>impressed</u> by your new advertising campaign.
*4* Our new product range has <u>beaten</u> the competition.

**2** Can you think of any other violent verbs that you could use in the sentences above?

**TOUGH TALK AND YOU**

Talk about these questions.

*1* If you met a negotiator with a similar attitude to Gekko's, how would you handle it? Would you try to be as tough as him? Would you try to be conciliatory? Or would you ignore his business style and behave as you always do? Explain.
*2* Tough talk is often considered to be 'macho' – or very male. Do you think that women have a different attitude to tough talk?

# doing business 1 *A proposal*

**THE SITUATION**

*Casablanca* is a film about a man called Rick (Humphrey Bogart) who owns a bar in the famous Moroccan city during World War Two. Everyone is looking for some 'letters of transit' which were stolen from government officials by a man called Aguardi. These letters are so valuable that Aguardi has already been killed because of them. In the scene below, Rick is approached by a rival bar owner called Signor Farrari, who believes that Rick now has the letters.

**CASABLANCA**

Read the script and answer these questions.

1  Is either Rick or Farrari upset about Aguardi's death?
2  What is the implication of the phrase '*Practically* no one'?
3  What is Farrari offering and what does he want in return?
4  How would you describe Rick's response to Farrari's proposal?

| | |
|---|---|
| FARRARI | Here, sit down. There's something I want to talk over with you anyhow. The news about Aguardi upsets me very much. |
| RICK | You're a fat hypocrite. You don't feel any sorrier for Aguardi than I do. |
| FARRARI | Of course not. What upsets me is that Aguardi is dead and no one knows where those letters of transit are. |
| RICK | Practically no one. |
| FARRARI | If I could lay my hands on those letters, I can make a fortune. |
| RICK | So could I and I'm a poor businessman. |
| FARRARI | I have a proposition for whoever has those letters. I'll handle the entire transaction, get rid of the letters, take all the risk, for a small percentage. |
| RICK | Are there carrying charges? |
| FARRARI | Naturally there'll be a few incidental expenses. That's the proposition I have for whoever has those letters. |
| RICK | I'll tell him when he comes in. |
| FARRARI | Rick, I'll put my cards on the table. I think you know where those letters are. |
| RICK | You're in good company. Renault and Strasser probably think so, too. That's why I came over here, to give them a chance to ransack my place. |
| FARRARI | Rick, don't be a fool, take me into your confidence. You need a partner. |
| RICK | Excuse me, I'll be getting back. |

*Humphrey Bogart as Rick in* Casablanca

**■ GLOSSARY ■**

hypocrite  *a person who says one thing and does another*

I'll tell him when he comes in.  *I'll tell this person when he visits my bar.*

Renault and Strasser  *two policemen who are looking for the letters of transit*

to ransack  *to search in a very thorough and destructive way*

**COLLOQUIAL LANGUAGE**

Both Rick and Farrari use colloquial language to discuss Farrari's proposal.

👥 Find phrases in the script which mean the same as the sentences in the box.

> If I could get those letters.
> I can make a lot of money.
> I'll be honest with you.
> You're not the only person with that opinion.
> Don't act unwisely.

**TALKING BUSINESS**

👥 The box contains some of the business terms that Rick and Farrari use. Match them to the definitions.

- the cost of storing things that have not yet been sold
- the process of making a payment
- a business idea or suggestion
- small amounts of money which are spent while doing the deal
- a very small part of the total amount of money exchanged

*proposition* *small percentage* *transaction* *incidental expenses* *carrying charges*

**REACTING POSITIVELY**

👥 How would you respond to Farrari's proposal more positively? Think of two possible responses in these situations. Then compare your ideas with the rest of the class.

*Situation 1*

You are keen to do business with Farrari and you want to start the meeting in a polite and friendly way. How would you reply to this?

FARRARI   Here, sit down. There's something I want to talk over with you anyhow. The news about Aguardi upsets me very much.

*Situation 2*

You have the valuable letters in your office. You are scared and want to sell them for the highest price as soon as possible. How would you reply to Farrari when he finishes explaining his proposition?

FARRARI   Naturally there'll be a few incidental expenses. That's the proposition I have for whoever has those letters.

*Situation 3*

Although you were suspicious at the start of the meeting, Farrari's proposition has persuaded you to do business with him. What would you say?

FARRARI   Rick, don't be a fool, take me into your confidence. You need a partner.

**PROPOSAL ROLES**

**1** 👥 Role play this situation.

**A** wants to sell a painting. **B** wants to sell a sports car.
**A** Offer to find a buyer for **B**'s sports car, in return for a small percentage of the price.
**B** Check exactly what **A** is proposing and respond positively.
**B** Offer to sell **A**'s painting in return for carrying charges and incidental expenses.
**A** Respond negatively.

**2** 👥 Each person should prepare a short business proposal to make to the other. The other person should respond as they think appropriate.

# doing **business** **2** *Negotiating tactics*

**KRUSCHEV'S THIRD SHOE**

During negotiations at the height of the Cold War, Americans were amazed when the Soviet leader Nikita Kruschev became so angry that he started banging his shoe on the table. However, photographs taken at the time show that while he did this, both of his shoes were still on his feet.

What does this tell you about Kruschev's negotiating tactics?

**TACTICS**

**1** Here are five tactics often used in negotiating. Match each tactic to its description below.

> The deadline
>
> Bullying
>
> Appeal to a higher authority
>
> Scarcity
>
> A last-minute claim

> saying that only your boss can offer the concession that is being asked for
>
> applying pressure by saying that you have to leave at a certain fixed time
>
> a demand which is made after it appears that agreement has been reached
>
> an aggressive demand for a concession to be made
>
> saying that this is your only chance to buy the product or service

**2** Which of these tactics do you think that Kruschev was using in the story above?

**FIVE NEGOTIATIONS**

Listen to five extracts from negotiations.

*1* For each extract decide which of the above tactics is being used.

*2* Listen again, and after each extract pause and talk about what is the best way to respond to the tactic.

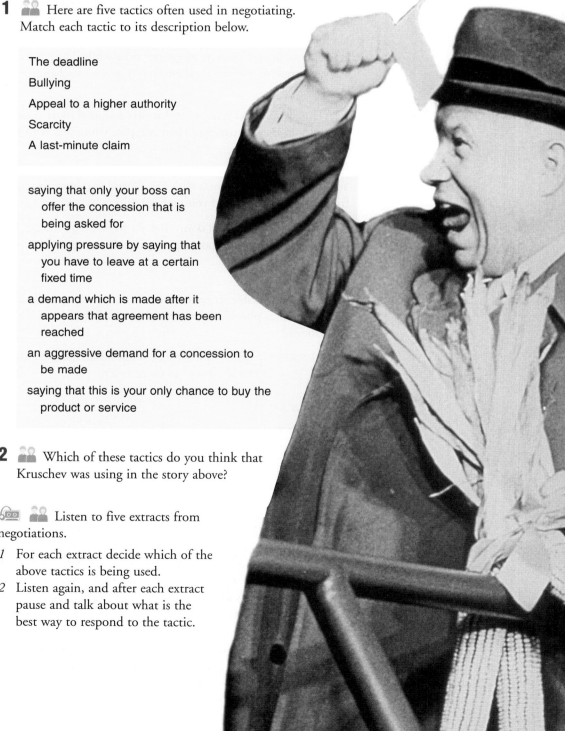

**FARGO**    In the movie *Fargo*, we see a car salesman called Jerry Lundegaard negotiating with a customer about the purchase of a new car. The customer is angry because he is being asked to pay for some TruCoat sealant, which he does not want.

**1**  Read the script and talk about these questions.

*1*  What is the customer's objective?
*2*  What is Jerry trying to get the customer to do?
*3*  Which of the tactics opposite are being used?

**2**  Here are three ways in which Jerry tries to avoid making a concession to the customer. Look again at the script and identify them.

▌ He justifies what's happened.
▌ He agrees with the customer.
▌ He explains why it's happened.

**3**  Who do you sympathise with more – Jerry or the customer?

| | |
|---|---|
| CUSTOMER | We sat right in this room and went over and over this. |
| JERRY | Yeah, but that TruCoat – |
| CUSTOMER | I sat right here and said I didn't want no TruCoat. |
| JERRY | Yeah, but I'm saying, that TruCoat, you don't get it and you get oxidization problems. It'll cost you a heck of a lot more than five hundred – |
| CUSTOMER | You're sitting here, you're talking in circles! You're talking like we didn't go over this already! |
| JERRY | Yeah, but this TruCoat – |
| CUSTOMER | We had us a deal here for nineteen-five. You sat there and darned if you didn't tell me you'd get this car, these options, without the sealant, for nineteen-five! |
| JERRY | OK, I'm not saying I didn't – |
| CUSTOMER | You called me twenty minutes ago and said you had it! Ready to make delivery, you says! Come on down and get it! And here you are and you're wasting my time and you're wasting my wife's time and I'm paying nineteen-five for this vehicle here! |

*William H. Macy as salesman Jerry*

JERRY    Well, OK, I'll talk to my boss. See, they install TruCoat at the factory, there's nothing we can do, but I'll talk to my boss.

▌ **GLOSSARY** ▌

oxidization    *rust (FeO$_2$)*
a heck of a lot more    *much, much more*
darned if you didn't    *you definitely did*
sealant    *a kind of paint that makes cars resistant to water damage*

**NEGOTIATING ROLES**    Use the role cards on page 125 (Student **A**) and page 126 (Student **B**) to have two negotiations. When appropriate, use the negotiating tactics on these pages and others that you know.

# issues

## *Negotiating tales*

Louis B. Mayer

**ARLEN'S LUCKY DAY**

**1** 🔊 👥 Listen to a story about a Hollywood scriptwriter called Michael Arlen and answer these questions.

*1* How successful was Michael Arlen?
*2* What advice did Sam Goldwyn give him?
*3* What did Louis B. Mayer offer him – and why?

**2** 👥 Talk about these questions.

*1* What would you have said to Louis B. Mayer in Michael Arlen's position?
*2* What lesson does the story teach about good negotiating?

Sam Goldwyn

**PICASSO'S SECRET ART**

👥 Read the story and discuss these questions.

*1* Could Rosenberg have handled the situation better? What would you have done?
*2* In what kind of situation *wouldn't* Picasso's tactic work?

At one time, the artist Pablo Picasso was represented by an art dealer called Paul Rosenberg. The two worked well together. Picasso produced his great masterpieces and Rosenberg sold them to wealthy collectors for enormous sums of money.

Then one day, for no obvious reason, Picasso called Rosenberg and told him that he would no longer work with him. Rosenberg was amazed. He felt that he had always done his best for Picasso and he had made him a great deal of money.

Picasso refused to give Rosenberg any explanation for his decision, but returned to his studio to work on his next masterpiece. Meanwhile, Rosenberg sat in his office and tried to make sense of what had happened. Had he done something wrong? Had someone else made Picasso a better offer? Surely he wasn't going to lose the greatest artist in the world?

After a number of sleepless nights, Rosenberg decided what to do. Tired and sick with worry, he paid a visit to the artist's studio.

'My dear friend,' said Rosenberg, 'I have a solution to our little problem. Why don't I simply increase the fee that I've been paying you?'

Picasso, of course, agreed.

## BISMARCK AND THE SAUSAGES

 Read the text and talk about these questions.

1 In what ways is this situation like a negotiation?
2 What lesson about good negotiating does it teach?

The German Chancellor Otto von Bismarck did not achieve the heights of power without making many enemies. One of his most persistent critics in the German parliament was a man called Rudolf Virchow, who was both a liberal politician and a doctor who specialised in the causes of disease.

One day, Bismarck decided that he'd had enough of Virchow's rude comments and he challenged the doctor to a duel. Virchow remained calm in the face of the challenge.

'As the Chancellor has asked for the duel,' he said, 'I believe that I have the choice of weapons.'

As this was the custom of the time, no one could disagree with Dr Virchow.

'In which case,' he said, 'I choose these!'

And the doctor produced two apparently identical sausages.

'One of these sausages,' he said, 'is infected with a deadly disease. The other is perfectly normal. In this duel, I will eat one and the Chancellor will eat the other. The Chancellor, of course, will have to guess which sausage is which.'

Bismarck immediately cancelled the challenge.

### ▌ GLOSSARY ▌

duel   *a fight between two people (normally with guns or swords) which often ends in the death of one person*

## NEGOTIATING AND YOU

Talk about how you would respond in each of the following situations. Do the three stories on these pages give you any ideas for approaching these negotiations?

You own a small farm that specialises in producing a certain kind of honey. 80% of your output is purchased by a large supermarket chain, which markets your products under its own label at a premium price. One day, the supermarket tells you that from now on it will pay 15% less for the honey that it buys from you – which means that your profit margin will be cut in half. What options do you have?

You are an antique dealer who has just acquired an extremely valuable seventeenth century Persian rug. Two wealthy collectors have already contacted you and said that they want to buy it from you. What's the best way for you to get the highest price?

You are an agent representing a talented young actress who is hoping to break into the film industry. A film director contacts you and offers her a big part in his new low-budget movie. To minimise his initial costs, the director is not paying any fees to his main actors, but is instead offering them a small percentage of any profits that the film might make. However, the actress you represent needs some money now. How can you get the best possible deal for her?

# 9 globalisation

> **globalisation** the tendency for the world economy to work as one unit, led by large international companies doing business all over the world
>
> Longman Business English Dictionary

**IS IT A MYTH?**  In his book *Great Myths of Business*, the business writer William Davis raises some doubts about the idea of globalisation.

Read the text and then do the following.

1  Summarise the five arguments for globalisation.
2  Can you think of twelve brands that are truly global? How soon is it before you hesitate?
3  Do you agree that globalisation is more myth than reality?

Theorists have spread the idea of 'globalisation' for years. We are all familiar with their arguments.

☞ Telecommunications and information technology have changed the world.

☞ Trade agreements have reduced protectionism.

☞ Capital flows more freely across borders.

☞ Television has made it possible to bring products and services to the attention of people everywhere.

☞ Big and powerful corporations operate in many different countries.

But just try asking marketing experts to name a dozen truly global brands. After a confident start they soon hesitate. The fact that we can drive the same car and communicate by telephone, fax or Internet does not necessarily mean that there is now a 'global shopping centre' where everyone buys the same things.

## IS IT ABOUT THE USA?

Anthony Giddens is the Director of the London School of Economics. In his book *Runaway World*, he tells this story about globalisation. Read the story and then talk about the questions below.

A friend of mine studies village life in central Africa. A few years ago she paid her first visit to a remote area. The day she arrived, she was invited to a local home for an evening's entertainment. She expected to find out about the traditional pastimes of this isolated community. Instead, the occasion turned out to be a viewing of *Basic Instinct* on video. The film at that point hadn't even reached the cinemas in London.

*1* Do you think that globalisation is just another way of describing the spread of American culture?
*2* Do you think that other countries or cultures are as important as America in the process of globalisation?
*3* Do you know any similar stories?

## OR IS IT REVOLUTION?

Tom Peters is one of the world's most influential management gurus. Read what he says about globalisation in *The Circle of Innovation* and then answer the questions below.

The global village is here. No business-person is, literally, more than six-tenths of a second (measured at the speed of light) away from any other businessperson. When I need a partner, I can just as easily look in Bangalore, India as next door in my Silicon Valley neighbourhood.

R.I.P. distance! Its passing means that services as varied as car design, home security and healthcare delivery will be as exportable as VCRs or automobiles. Airlines such as Swissair and British Airways are already sending their back office work to India.

We are in the midst of the most profound change since the beginning of the Industrial Revolution over two centuries ago.

### ▌ GLOSSARY ▌

R.I.P.  *rest in peace (a phrase often used with reference to dead people)*

VCR  *video cassette recorder*

back office work  *administration and support work*

*1* Why is the speed of light now important for businesspeople?
*2* How can car design, home security and healthcare delivery be exported?
*3* How can European airlines now do back office work in India?
*4* What do you think? Are we really in the middle of the biggest change since the Industrial Revolution?

## GLOBALISATION AND YOU

Discuss these questions.

*1* What kind of impact has globalisation had on your life?
*2* What positive or negative effects of globalisation have you noticed?
*3* Which of the views in the three texts you've read do you think is closest to the truth?

# G R A M M A R   R E V I E W

**BLACK WEDNESDAY**

Black Wednesday is the name given to the day in 1992 when the British government fought the world's currency speculators – and lost! The result was that the British pound was forced to leave the European Exchange Rate Mechanism (ERM), the system that led to the establishment of the euro.

Listen to the first part of the report on Black Wednesday and answer these questions.

*1* Who was Norman Lamont?
*2* What did he announce on Black Wednesday?
*3* Why was this such bad news for John Major's government?
*4* Complete this third conditional sentence.

> If Black Wednesday had never happened, Tony Blair _____ never have become prime minister.

*5* Which other words in the box can you use in the sentence above and keep roughly the same meaning?

**could  might  would  should  must**

'Today has been an extremely difficult and turbulent day. Massive speculative flows have continued to disrupt the functioning of the Exchange Rate Mechanism. The government has concluded that Britain's best interests are served by suspending our membership of the Exchange Rate Mechanism.'  *Norman Lamont*

**THIRD CONDITIONALS**

Put the verbs in brackets into the correct form to complete these sentences. In each case, you'll need to choose an appropriate word from the box above.

*1* Without John Major's agreement, Norman Lamont _____ (not take) the decision to leave the ERM.
*2* If it _____ (not be) such a turbulent day on the currency markets, the pound _____ (not leave) the ERM.
*3* The pound _____ (remain) in the ERM if it _____ (be) a much calmer day on the currency markets.
*4* If John Major's government _____ (recover), he _____ (win) the next election.
*5* Black Wednesday _____ (not be) so important if the ERM _____ (not be) such a key part of government policy.

> ### ▌ CHECK
>
> The **third conditional** is used to speculate about things in the past which didn't happen.
>
> *If Black Wednesday had never happened, Tony Blair might never have become prime minister.*
>
> ▌ *For more on the third conditional, see page 130.* ▌

# Conditional 3

## THE MAN WHO BROKE THE POUND

*George Soros*

**1** 🔊 👥 Listen to the second part of the recording and answer these questions.

1  How much money did George Soros borrow?
2  What was the pound – Deutschmark exchange rate before and after Black Wednesday?
3  How much did Black Wednesday cost the British people?

**2** 🔊 Listen again and complete these sentences.

If it hadn't been for Black Wednesday, George Soros ...
He explained what would have happened if ...
Had I not (= *If I hadn't*) taken the position, someone else ...

## MORE SPECULATIONS

👥 Use these notes to make up third conditional sentences.

1  The pound had to leave the ERM, but if the pound stay / Soros not make so much
2  Soros wasn't worried about his gamble, but if be worried / not take such a big risk
3  Soros thought that the pound was a 'one-way bet', so if be wrong / not lose too much money
4  Soros didn't feel guilty, but if feel guilty / act differently
5  In Soros's position, I ...

## SUCCESS, FAILURE AND YOU

👥 What do you consider to be your greatest success or failure? Think about the steps that led up to it. Make up a few sentences that explain what might have happened if you hadn't taken those steps.

# *International finance*

**THE ASIA CRISIS**

In 1997, the international financial system was plunged into chaos by a chain of events which started in Thailand and sent currency markets falling around the world. In the text opposite, the humorous American writer P. J. O'Rourke explains what happened.

**ECONOMIC INDICATORS**

Before you read the text, look at the six indicators in the box which tell you about the health of a country's economy. Match each indicator to one of the words or phrases in the box.

▮ rising prices
▮ people out of work
▮ loans
▮ currency
▮ share prices
▮ imports and exports

**exchange rate**   *stock market index*
**unemployment rate**   **inflation**
**balance of payments**   interest rate

**THE 97 BULL MARKET**

Read section **1** of the text and do the following.

*1* Explain the joke about the dog and McDonald's.
*2* Why were Asian economies doing so well in early 1997? Find two reasons.

**STABBING THE BAHT**

Read section **2** and answer these questions.

*1* Why did currency traders think it was a good idea to sell the baht? Find at least two reasons.
*2* Look closely at this section and find the following.

▮ a phrase meaning 'currency'
▮ the opposite of 'surplus'
▮ a loan that might not be repaid
▮ a loan that definitely won't be repaid
▮ another word for 'shares'

**GOVERNMENT ACTION**

**1** Before you read section **3**, discuss this question.

When a country's currency starts falling in value, how can the government defend it?

**2** Read section **3** and answer these questions.

*1* Did the Thai government take the kind of action you expected?
*2* Why don't governments like devaluation?
*3* In currency trading, what is 'selling short'?

**THE TERROR**

**1** Before you read section **4**, use your general knowledge to say what these terms are.

*Dow Jones* **Hang Seng** won *ringgit* rupiah

**2** Read section **4** and do the following.

*1* List the countries or areas through which the crisis spread.
*2* What is O'Rourke's explanation for the fall in the value of the American dollar?

# THE ASIA CRISIS

**1** Back in 1997, there'd been a bull market since the time of the dinosaurs. The unemployment rate was so low that if your dog wandered into a McDonald's, it would wander out wearing a trainee badge. And Asian economies were even stronger than America's. They had some kind of 'Asian values' thing going on, involving hard work, thrift and respect for the family. Plus, countries in Asia had smart government policies such as 'Export everything'. The world was getting calculators, stereos and VCRs. Asians were getting rich. Everything was wonderful.

**2** Then somebody attacked the baht. Currency traders snuck up behind Thailand's legal tender and stabbed it with a chicken satay skewer. What currency traders really did to the baht was to sell it. Investors in international currency markets started looking at Thailand's economy. Maybe the world had as many calculators, stereos and VCRs as it wanted. But the Thais were borrowing overseas to produce more – borrowing so much money that Thailand had a balance of payments deficit even though it was exporting everything. Thailand had risky debt, bad debt and worse equities. Maybe owning baht wasn't such a good idea.

**3** Currency traders sold baht. The government of Thailand bought baht, using the foreign currency it had from exporting calculators, stereos and VCRs. Thailand did this to keep the baht from being devalued. Devaluation simply means admitting your currency is worth less compared with other currencies, but no government likes to do it. When a currency is devalued, imported raw materials become more expensive.

Inflation rises. Stock prices fall. Everything goes in the toilet. Anyway, currency traders were glad to sell baht, so they sold some more. Aggressive currency traders even sold baht they didn't own. They borrowed baht to sell, hoping to repay the loan later with cheaper baht. (This is called 'selling short'.)

**4** When the currency traders were done with Thailand, they started looking at other economies in Asia. Maybe owning Indonesian rupiah, Malaysian ringgit and South Korean won wasn't such a good idea either. By October 1997, the currency-dumping spree had reached Hong Kong. The Hang Seng index fell 1211 points on October 23, with its shares losing $42 billion in value. This scared the pants off the Japanese market. The Japanese shocked the European markets, which took it out on Mexico and Brazil. By Monday October 27, the terror had reached the New York Stock Exchange. The Dow Jones industrial average went down 554 points because ... because everyone else was doing it. It was the largest dollar decline in history and the largest percentage drop in ten years.

### ▌ GLOSSARY ▌

skewer   *a stick on which food is cooked*
thrift   *careful use of money*
to sneak up behind   *to surprise*
to be done with   *to finish with*
currency-dumping spree   *an intense period of selling currency*
to scare the pants off   *to terrify*
to take it out on   *to express anger against*

Eat the Rich *by P. J. O'Rourke*

---

**THE WORLD ECONOMY AND YOU**

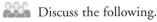 Discuss the following.

*1* If you were a currency trader, would you attack your country's currency at the moment? Explain why – or why not?

*2* In what ways is it a *good* thing that national economies around the world are now linked so closely together?

# doing **business 1** *Travel*

**THE JET AGE**   In his book *Company Man* Anthony Sampson talks about the development of business travel in the 1960s and 70s. Read the text and talk about the questions below.

By the early sixties, there was a new kind of company man. He could fly non-stop across the Atlantic in seven hours; he could stay in a foreign country for only one night, at a hotel which looked exactly the same as one at home; he could talk to his office or his wife without delay by direct-dial telephone.

He was more widely travelled than any earlier businessman, but compared to those slower travellers, he had limitations. His real experience of other countries was much more limited; he was more insulated from their inhabitants; and the further he travelled, the more he was dependent on his company.

In the early jet age, some company doctors still insisted that executives should take a day off after a long flight, to avoid the disorientation of jet-lag; and some companies encouraged transatlantic travellers to return by sea to re-orientate themselves. But by the seventies most businessmen took the acceleration of travel for granted.

1   The text talks only about company men (because there were few women business travellers in the 1960s and 1970s). But are there any reasons why this lifestyle should be more appealing to men than to women?

2   Do you agree that modern business travellers have more limitations than business travellers of the past? Explain.

3   Do you think it would still be a good idea if business travellers returned from long journeys by ship?

4   How has the experience of business travel changed since the 1960s and 1970s? Make a list of differences between then and now.

**TRAVEL ROLES** 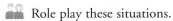 Role play these situations.

**A** You are on a plane and you want to talk to the person next to you about your most recent travel experience. Try to start a conversation.

**B** You are coming back from a tiring trip and you want to go to sleep. Be polite to your partner, but try to indicate that you'd rather be left in peace.

**B** This is only your second business trip and you are in the departures lounge of an airport. It has just been announced that your flight will be delayed by three hours. Turn to the person sitting next to you and start a conversation.

**A** You have been travelling on business for the past twenty years and you have seen it all before. Talk about how much things have (or haven't) changed in that time.

**ARRIVING** Iain Banks's novel *The Business* tells the story of a businesswoman called Kathryn Telman. Read this description of her arrival at the airport in Karachi, Pakistan and talk about 1–3 below.

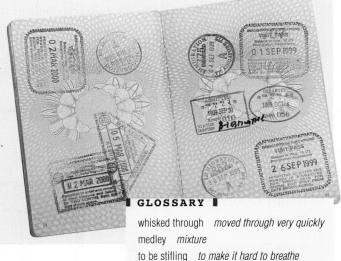

I had a feeling that whatever passport I chose for Karachi, it would be the wrong one, but I decided on the British one and was pleasantly surprised; whisked through. The place was packed, the air was thick with a medley of smells, the humidity was stifling and the lighting in the arrivals hall was terrible. Over the crowds I spotted a board being held up with a rough approximation of my name on it.

'Mrs Telman,' said the young Pakistani man holding the sign up. 'I am Mo Meridalawah. Very pleased to meet you.'

'It's Ms Telman, but thank you. How do you do?'

'Very well, thank you. Let me ...' He took my bags off me. 'Follow me, please. This way.'

**GLOSSARY**

whisked through   *moved through very quickly*
medley   *mixture*
to be stifling   *to make it hard to breathe*

*1* Why does Kathryn say 'Ms Telman'?

*2* When Kathryn says 'How do you do?', Mo Meridalawah doesn't give the standard English response. What would you expect him to say?

*3* Compare Kathryn's experience of arriving at Karachi with your most recent experience of arriving at an airport. (Think about passport control and customs, the atmosphere of the airport, how you managed the next stage of your journey, etc.)

**ARRIVAL ROLES** Role play these situations.

**A** You are an experienced business traveller, arriving in a country for the first time. You are expecting to be met by the head of your company's local office.

**B** You know nothing about **A**'s business but have been asked by your friend to pick him/her up from the airport because your friend is sick. Introduce yourself, explain the situation and have a brief conversation.

**A** You are the boss of the subsidiary of a large multinational and you have decided to meet a new employee of the parent company at the airport, because you are suspicious about the motives for his/her trip. Welcome **B** and have a brief conversation.

**B** You've only been working for the company for three weeks and have been sent out to write a secret report on the subsidiary's activities. You've had a difficult journey and you're feeling very tired.

# doing business 2 *Using humour*

**JOKES AND CULTURE**

Richard D. Lewis is an expert on doing business in different cultures. This is what he writes about the advantages of using humour in international business situations.

> The introduction of humour in international business talks may bring considerable gain in terms of breaking the ice, speeding up the issues, escaping from deadlock, putting your partners at ease and winning their confidence in you as a human being.
>
> *When Cultures Collide by Richard D. Lewis*

 Discuss these questions.

1  Do you agree with Richard's list of the advantages of using humour? What other advantages can you add to it?
2  What do you think are the disadvantages of using humour in international business situations?

**AN EXPENSIVE JOKE**

 Read this story about a joke that went wrong and then talk about the questions below.

**T**he British are supposed to be famous for laughing at themselves. But even their sense of humour has a limit, as the British retailer Gerald Ratner found out to his cost.

When Ratner took over his father's chain of 130 jeweller's shops in 1984, he introduced a very clear company policy. He decided that his shops should sell down-market products at the lowest possible prices. It was a great success. The British public loved his cheap gold earrings and his tasteless silver ornaments. By 1991, Ratner's company had 2,400 shops and it was worth over £680 million.

But in April of that year, Gerald Ratner made a big mistake. At a big meeting of top British businesspeople, he stood up and explained the secret of his success: 'People say, how can we sell our goods for such a low price? I say, because they're absolute rubbish.'

His audience roared with laughter. But the British newspapers and the British public were not so amused. People felt insulted and stayed away from Ratners' shops. Sales slumped and six months after his speech Ratners' share price had fallen by 42%. The following year, things got worse and Gerald Ratner was forced to resign. By the end of 1992 he'd lost his company, his career and his house. Even worse, 25,000 of his employees had lost their jobs.

It had been a very expensive joke.

1  Would people in your country have found Gerald Ratner's joke funny?
2  Do you think that Gerald Ratner deserved what happened to him?
3  Can you think of a similar story from business or personal life when a joke has gone badly wrong?

**BUSINESS ONE-LINERS**

**1** Here are some one-liners (short jokes) typical of British business life. All of them make fun of people. Which of these jokes is told at the expense of ...

▌ someone who is bad at business?
▌ someone who is very unemotional?
▌ someone who is very boring?
▌ a person who is always trying to please others?
▌ the person who is telling the joke?

> Sorry that Terry can't be with us today – he's not feeling too good. He was washing the boss's car when his tongue ran dry.

> Should you go into business with her? Well, let's put it this way, if she went into the funeral business, no one would die.

> He may seem like a tough guy, but he's really very sentimental. In fact, he's got the heart of a little boy – he keeps it in a jar next to his bed.

> Yes, we certainly have a bad education system in this country. The problem is that 50% of the people can't read properly, 50% can't write properly and the other 50% can't add up.

> She'd make a great governor of the Bank of England. Whenever she speaks, everyone's interest rate drops.

*Adapted from* One-Liners for Business Speeches *by Mitch Murray*

**2** 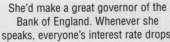 Talk about these questions.

*1* Are there any jokes which you don't understand? Find someone in the group to explain them to you.
*2* Which do you think are amusing? Are there any which you think are offensive?

**TELLING A JOKE**

**1**  Listen to the joke on the recording.

**2** Take turns to tell each other a joke. (If you can't remember any, tell your version of the joke that you just heard on the recording.)

# issues

## *Working in other cultures*

**CULTURAL
DIFFERENCES**

This is the kind of advice that you'll often find in books on doing business in other cultures. Look at the advice and then talk about the questions below.

*In Russia, it's bad manners to ask where the toilet is.*

**When you finish a meal in China, always leave some food on your plate. A completely empty plate is a sign that you want more.**

*Remember that people often nod their head for 'No' in Bulgaria.*

**Don't eat food with your left hand when in the Arab world.**

1 Would you like to be given this kind of information before a business trip? Why – or why not?
2 Can you think of any customs or traditions that are typical of your country? If a foreign businessperson didn't know about them, how important would it be?

**CULTURAL
SIMILARITIES**

Read this American writer's description of the way that people behave in elevators (lifts) and then talk about the questions below.

It has been proved by scientists using hidden cameras that when only one or two people ride in an elevator, they usually lean against the walls. If four people are aboard, they usually move towards the four corners. However, when the population reaches five or six people, everyone begins to obey more complex rules of elevator etiquette. It is almost like a ritualistic dance. They all turn to face the door. 'They get taller and thinner,' as psychologist Layne Longfellow describes it. 'Hands and purses hang down in front of the body. They mustn't touch each other in any way unless the elevator is crowded and then only lightly at the shoulder or upper arm. Also there is a tendency to look upward at the illuminated floor indicator. If they speak, it is definitely sotto voce.'

*Do's and Taboos of Humor around the World
by Roger E. Axtell*

**▌ GLOSSARY ▌**

purse (US)   *handbag (UK)*
sotto voce   *an Italian phrase that means 'quietly'*

1 In your experience, do people behave in the same way in lifts all around the world?
2 Can you think of other examples of situations where people behave in the same way all over the world? (Think about things like the way people behave in supermarket queues or in airport departure lounges.)

**CULTURE SHOCK**  When people have a strong reaction to their experience of another country, they often talk about 'culture shock'. This can lead to a variety of problems – from headaches to emotional troubles.

 Read this story about an American businessman and then talk about the questions below.

I was a 45-year-old American and had come to Asia to work on a three-year assignment. Although I saw myself as a very sociable and adaptable man, my work pattern became erratic, which was noted by the company. I would be late and sometimes not turn up at all – at other times I seemed to work around the clock. My colleagues seemed to be used to the 'eccentric' behaviour of foreigners and did not think too much about it.

After six months, I fetched a boat to an island in a neighbouring country; on arrival, I took off my clothes and threatened the local population with a gun in a stark-naked state. Eventually, I gave myself up to the police and was sent back to my home country. It was clear that I could not stay abroad and function in my job – I returned home to recover.

Breaking Through Culture Shock *by Elisabeth Marx*

1  What action do you think the company should have taken after the businessman's arrest?
2  Does culture shock excuse the businessman's behaviour?
3  What action do you think the police would have taken if the naked man with the gun had been a poor local person?
4  Have you ever suffered from culture shock? If so, how did it affect you?
5  How would you try to avoid the effects of culture shock when travelling?

**CULTURE AND YOU**   Discuss these questions.

1  Which of these kinds of behaviour would you consider 'erratic' or 'eccentric'?

▌ arriving late in the morning
▌ working until late in the evening
▌ singing in the office
▌ appearing distracted or sleepy in meetings
▌ wearing clothes that don't match
▌ missing deadlines
▌ drinking alcohol at lunch
▌ being aggressive to subordinates

2  What other examples of erratic or eccentric behaviour have you seen in the workplace?
3  Do you think that people from other cultures would agree with you on what is erratic or eccentric behaviour? Give examples.

# 10 vision

**ROCKET ROLLERS**

Every businessperson would like to have a vision of a new product or a new service that would change the way that we all live.

 Look at the man in the photograph and then discuss these questions.

1  What's his vision?
2  What are the good points about this idea?
3  Why do you think it wasn't a success?
4  In the past ten years, which new products or services have changed the way we live?

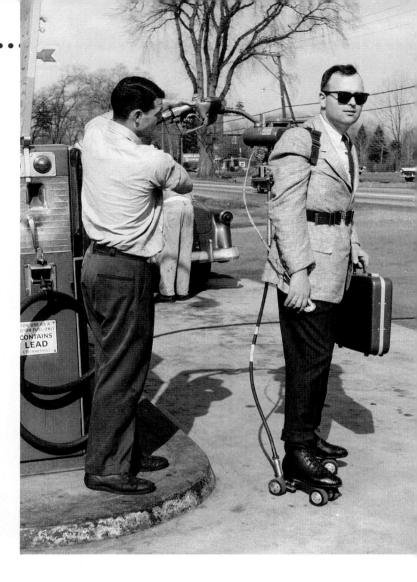

**WHO IS THE BUSINESS VISIONARY?**

Read the three texts and discuss the questions.

## The Manager

Three stonecutters were asked what they were doing.

The first replied, 'I am making a living.'

The second replied, 'I am doing the best job of stonecutting in the country.'

The third replied, 'I am building a cathedral.'

The third man is, of course, the true 'manager'.

*Peter Drucker, business guru*

## The Unreasonable Man

The reasonable man adapts himself to the world. The unreasonable man persists in trying to adapt the world to himself. Therefore, all progress depends on the unreasonable man.

*George Bernard Shaw, Irish writer*

## The Entrepreneur

The entrepreneur Philip Villers explained his secret of success like this:

'Unreasonable commitment based upon inadequate evidence.'

1  In what sense do you think a manager can be a visionary?
2  What type of person do you think Shaw had in mind?
3  Can you think of any times in your life when you have acted with unreasonable commitment based upon inadequate evidence? Explain.
4  What kind of people do you think are the real visionaries in business? Give examples.

## PAST AND PRESENT VISIONS

Read this article about how new technology has changed our lives in unexpected ways and then discuss the questions below.

New technologies have always changed the world in unforeseeable ways. Who could have imagined when the first car rolled along a road, how that invention would alter shopping, urban design or courtship? When Faraday experimented with electricity, who foresaw the coming of the skyscraper, its lifts driven by electrical power, or the movement of women into the workplace, their domestic productivity transformed by the washing machine and the vacuum cleaner? What connection did anyone make between the arrival of television and the future of political debate or of branded goods? It is a cliche to say that 'the Internet changes everything': the challenge now is to guess what, how and how quickly.

*The Economist 26.6.99*

1 How has the car changed shopping, urban design and courtship over the past hundred years?

2 What is the connection between Michael Faraday's experiments with electricity and working women?

3 How do you think that TV has changed political debate over the past fifty years?

4 Look into the future. What unexpected long-term effects do you think that the growth of the Internet could have? Think of at least two.

5 Do you have any visions for future products that could change the way we live?

# GRAMMAR REVIEW

**THE MOST POWERFUL BUSINESSWOMAN**

Carly Fiorina was named as the most powerful businesswoman in America by *Fortune* magazine in both 1998 and 1999. This is the story of how she got her job as boss of the computer company Hewlett-Packard.

**1** Read the article and do the following.

*1* Find three reasons that the article gives for why she got the job.
*2* Which sentence in the article uses reported speech?
*3* What do you think were the original words used in that example of reported speech?

When Carly Fiorina was competing to become the new CEO of Hewlett-Packard, she stood out not because she was a woman, but because she had never worked in the computer industry. How did she handle it?

'Look, lack of computer expertise is not Hewlett-Packard's problem,' she remembers telling HP's directors. 'There are loads of people here who can provide that. You have deep engineering prowess. I bring strategic vision, which HP needs.'

Besides making a forceful sales pitch, Fiorina identified a key member of the HP board who could be her ally and partner: Dick Hackborn. In her second meeting with Hackborn, Fiorina said that if she became CEO, she wanted him to be chairman.

'This came as a complete surprise,' says Hackborn, 62. But after checking with fellow directors, he agreed to be chairman – for a while.

'This job won't last long,' he says. 'Carly is 90% of the partnership and she has all the capabilities to be an outstanding leader of HP.'

**▌ GLOSSARY ▌**

prowess   *knowledge and skill*
ally   *supporter*

*Fortune 25.10.99*

**2** Summarise the article by completing these sentences.

*1* *Fortune* magazine asked Fiorina how ...
*2* Fiorina told HP's directors that lack of computer expertise ...
*3* Hackborn said that Fiorina's offer ...
*4* He said that his job as chairman ...
*5* He explained that Fiorina ...

**▌ CHECK**

When we **report speech** using a past verb, we normally put the tense of the verb(s) in the other clause one tense back in the past.

*'I bring strategic vision,' she said.*
*She said she brought strategic vision.*

▌ *For more on this point, turn to page 145.* ▌

# *Reporting speech*

**SUMMARISING HITE**

Shere Hite's book *Sex and Business* talks about the way that men and women behave in the workplace. Read these extracts from her interviews with the bosses of some of the world's top corporations. Then take it in turns to put each question into reported speech and make a brief summary of each reply. Where appropriate, use the summarising verbs in the box.

*explain* **claim** *insist* point out assure suggest

*Hite asked Gauer what he thought of the slogan 'preservation of family values'. In reply Gauer suggested that the phrase had lost its old meaning. He claimed that today many executives have two families and pointed out that many executives spend far more time with their working family than with their private family.*

HITE — What do you think of the slogan 'preservation of family values'?

GAUER — What are 'family values' really? Many executives today have two families – a working family where you spend eight or nine hours and a private family with whom you spend much less time. One hour in the morning when you wake up and are in a bad mood anyway, and one hour at the end of the day when you are dead tired. This can make for a tumultuous day!

*Jean Jacques Gauer, CEO, Leading Hotels of the World, Switzerland*

HITE — Why aren't there women in the top jobs?

CEBRIAN — There is a problem with women's attitude in the labour market. They don't fight enough for power. Quite often they are better than men, but they choose not to fight, they choose to focus on family, especially the kids, while men focus on power and work.

*Juan Luis Cebrian, chairman of the media conglomerate, PRISA, Spain*

HITE — How are changes in the Japanese family affecting people who work for you?

OGINO — The social system and the family are changing now, but these changes are not finished, of course. I sometimes wonder where they are going ... Today 25% of marriages in Japan end in divorce, and those divorces are mostly initiated by women. We have not had a phenomenon like this in Japan before, with many young women saying they would prefer not to marry and continue to work.

*Naoki Ogino, boss of the Japanese newspaper, Yomiuri Shimbun*

HITE — If there were a return to family values, would less women work, therefore creating more full employment?

FRITZ — This is not the way to approach the future. We must keep women's options to work open, just as we do men's. Anyway, the definition of work is changing. In the future, those with regular eight-hour employment will be in a minority; most others will work independently for various companies or as part-time employees.

*Laurenz Fritz, Austrian Minister for Industry*

HITE — Do the media have the right to look at the private life of a figure like Clinton?

GIULIANI — Somebody's private life is only relevant when it affects their public life; this should not be an excuse for voyeurism. People or the press can be fascinated with a famous figure's private life, when it has no relevance to his or her job.

*Rudolph Giuliani, mayor of New York City*

**SEX, BUSINESS AND YOU**

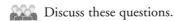

Discuss these questions.

*1* Do you strongly agree or disagree with the answers given by the businesspeople above? Explain why.

*2* How would you have answered Shere Hite's five questions?

# *Opportunity and invention*

**vocabulary**

**NEW BUSINESS**

Kevin Kelly is one of the world's leading writers on the effects of digital technology on the economy. The text opposite comes from his book *New Rules for the New Economy*.

👥 The four words in the box have similar meanings. Before you read the text, match them to the four definitions below.

**invention    opportunity    niche    innovation**

▮ the chance to do something successfully
▮ something which is made or designed for the first time
▮ the chance to sell a product or service aimed at a group of people with particular needs
▮ a product or idea which is better than something similar that came before

**THE ONGOING ECONOMY**

👥 In his book, Kevin Kelly uses this diagram to illustrate the way that opportunities are created in the modern world. Read section **1** of the text and explain what the diagram shows.

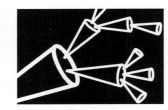

**NET WORDS**

👥 Read section **2** of the text and do the following.

*1* Explain why it is so cheap to advertise on the Internet.
*2* Find someone in the class who can explain each of these Net terms.

**posting    home page    link    news group    programmer**

**SCAVENGERS AND SPAMMERS**

**1** 👥 Before you read section **3** of the text, decide which of the words in the box is not normally associated with the digital world.

**bot    scavenger bot    junk mail    spammer**

**2** 👥 Read section **3** and do the following.

*1* Use the text to help you to understand what each of the words in the box means. Then take turns to explain them to each other.
*2* Explain how people make money from scavenger bots.

**THE ANTI-SPAM BOT**

**1** 👥 Before you read section **4**, think of at least one example of an Internet access company or Internet provider.

**2** 👥 Read section **4** and answer these questions.

*1* Why do Internet access companies want to stop spammers?
*2* How do they find out where spam is coming from?

**OTHER OPPORTUNITIES**

**1** 👥 Summarise the text by explaining how the invention of e-mail led to the anti-spam bot.

**2** 👥👥 What other problems and opportunities has the Internet created for business? Think of at least two and then compare your ideas with other groups.

**1** A steady stream of human attention and thought is applied to inventing new tools, devising new amusements and creating new wants. But no matter how small, each innovation is a platform for yet other innovations to launch from. It is this expanding space of opportunities that creates an ongoing economy. Like a chain reaction, one innovation can trigger dozens, if not hundreds, of other innovations down the line.

**2** Consider, for example, e-mail. E-mail is a recent invention that has ignited a frenzy of innovation and opportunity. Unlike a piece of ordinary mail, an e-mail advertisement costs exactly the same to send to one person or one million people – assuming you have a million addresses. Where does one get a million addresses? People innocently post their addresses all over the Net – at the bottom of their home page, or in a posting on a news group, or in a link off an article. These postings suggested an open opportunity to programmers.

**3** One of them came up with the idea of a scavenger bot. (A bot, short for robot, is a small bit of code.) A scavenger bot roams the Net looking for any phrase containing the e-mail @ sign. When it finds a phrase containing @, the scavenger bot assumes it is an address, so it collects it and then compiles a list of these addresses. These lists are then sold for $20 per thousand to spammers – the folks who mail unsolicited ads (junk mail) to huge numbers of recipients.

**4** The birth of scavenger bots suddenly created niches for anti-spam bots. Companies that sell Internet access want to protect their customers from spam, so they put false e-mail addresses on the Net. When these addresses are picked up by scavenger bots and used by spammers, the Internet provider receives mail which it can track to find out where the spam is coming from. Then the provider blocks the spam from that source for all their customers, which keeps everyone happy and loyal.

**▍ GLOSSARY ▍**

to trigger *to start*    to ignite *to start*    frenzy *mad activity*
scavenger *an animal like a hyena that eats things that other animals don't want*
to roam *to move around*    unsolicited *not requested*    to track *to follow*

# doing business 1   *Presentations 1*

**INTRODUCTION**

Management guru Tom Peters is one of the most successful presenters in the business world. He is also one of the most highly paid, sometimes earning over $50,000 for one presentation. Here is a chance to analyse his presentation technique, using extracts from a talk he gave to an audience of leading British businesspeople and politicians.

**STARTING A PRESENTATION**

**1** Which of the following would you expect to hear at the beginning of a business presentation? Why?

▌ the purpose of the presentation      ▌ a story
▌ a joke      ▌ the most important point
▌ a plan of the presentation

**2** Listen to Extract 1, the start of Tom Peters' presentation. Is this the kind of start you expected?

**TOM PETERS' START**

**1** Listen again and fill in the gaps in the script with the words and phrases in the box.

> the science of management
> a pleasure
> market share
> the real world
> a most dubious distinction

Good evening. It's (1) _____ to be here with you. Ian, in his remarks, referred kindly to me as one of the quote 'numerous breed of American students of (2) _____'. I am afraid that I would view that frankly as (3) _____ . It is a little discussed fact that America's (4) _____ has increased in management consulting, business school graduates and management publications exactly at the time that our market share in (5) _____ of hard goods and services has decreased.

▌ **GLOSSARY** ▌

Ian    *the name of the person who has just introduced him*

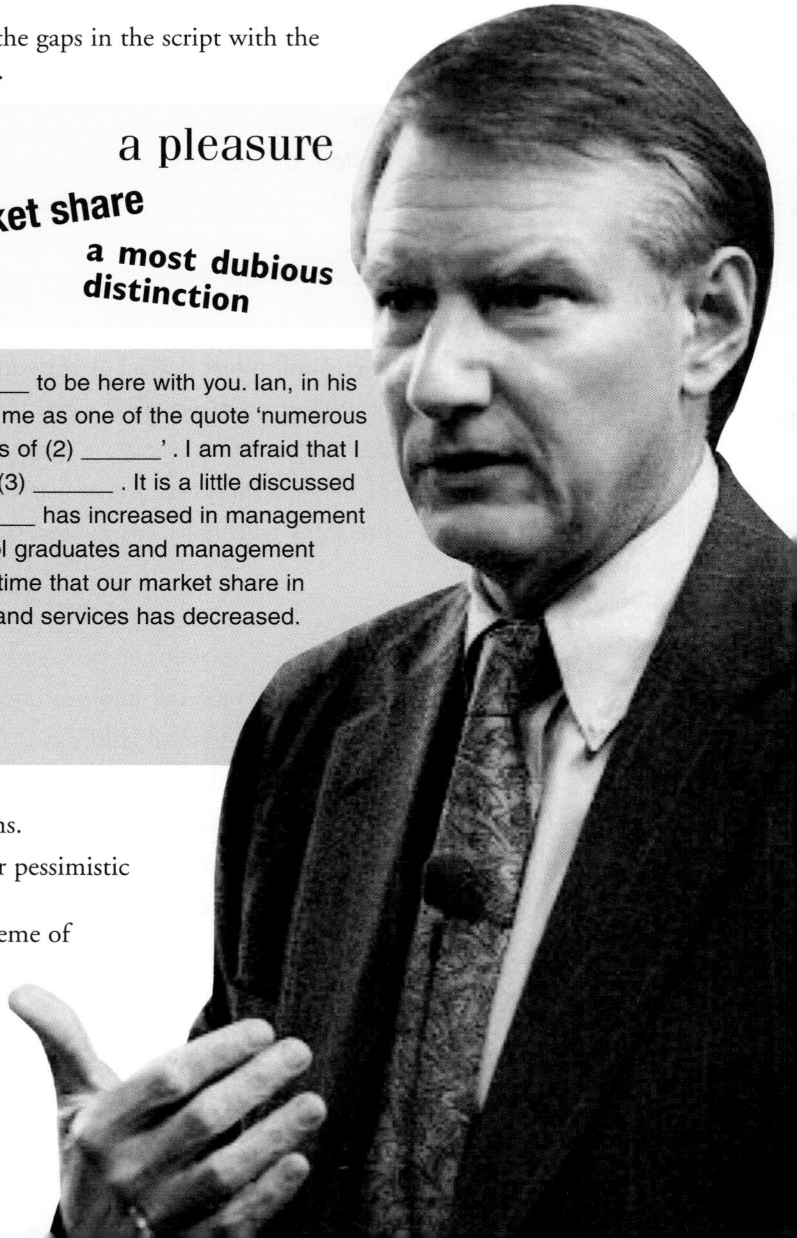

**2** Talk about these questions.

*1* Is Tom Peters optimistic or pessimistic about business?
*2* What do you think the theme of the presentation will be?

**INNOVATION**   Listen to Extract 2, in which Peters talks about innovation, and answer these questions.

*1* What kind of person does Peters say we depend on for innovation and progress?

*2* 'Unreasonable commitment based upon inadequate evidence.' What is this sentence a definition of?

*3* What do you think of the way that Peters delivers this part of the presentation? Do you think it is effective – or is it too theatrical? Explain your opinions.

**EMPHASIS**

**1** Read this script of part of Extract 2. Underline one or two words in each sentence which you think are most important and should be emphasised.

> ... we totally depend on irrational people. I mean, the reality is that the odds of a successful innovation making it to market are zero. Therefore, if you were a so-called expected-value thinker, you would never start. We depend on people who see the world irrationally.

**▌ GLOSSARY ▐**

odds *chances*

expected-value thinker *a person who logically calculates the chances of success*

**2** Take turns to deliver this part of the presentation to the rest of the group, emphasising the words you underlined. In each presentation, others in the group should say which words the speaker underlined.

**3** Listen to Tom Peters' performance of this part of the presentation again. Which words does he emphasise? Do you prefer your version or his? Explain why.

**PAUSING**

**1** Read this script of the end of Extract 2. Put a mark where you think you should pause.

> And that again is deadly serious. That's what we're dealing with, that's what we're talking about and it is the antithesis of the way we typically run our businesses.

**▌ GLOSSARY ▐**

antithesis *complete opposite*

**2** Take turns to deliver this part of the presentation to the rest of the group, pausing at the places you have marked.

**3** Compare your version with the way that Tom Peters delivers this part of the presentation.

**PAUSING AND EMPHASIS**

**1** Mark the script for this part of Peters' presentation for both emphasis and pauses.

> 'The reasonable man adapts himself to the world. The unreasonable man persists in trying to adapt the world to himself. Therefore, all progress depends on the unreasonable man.'
> No problem, except we go out of our way to fire unreasonable men within all of our organisations.

**2** Take turns to deliver this part of the presentation to your partner.

**3** Compare your version with the original.

# doing business 2 *Presentations 2*

**RHETORIC**

Rhetoric is the ancient art of persuasive speaking. Tom Peters uses a number of rhetorical devices in his presentations. Here we look at a few of them as he continues his presentation.

**INTRODUCING THE THEME**

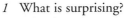 Listen to Extract 3 of his presentation. Which of these sentences summarises the real point that he is making?

▮ Companies should worry about the fluctuation of the oil price.
▮ Companies should eliminate ambiguity and uncertainty from their thinking.
▮ Companies need to return to the old ideas of Henry Ford.
▮ Companies should reorganise so that they are ready for the changes of the modern world.

**HUMOUR AND SURPRISE**

Listen to the first part of Extract 3 again. Then look at the script and talk about the questions below.

> You hear it here first tonight. I am that rare person in the world who is able to predict with certainty the price of oil next year at this time. I will personally guarantee you that it will either be seven or forty-seven dollars a barrel. I will likewise guarantee you that if it's forty-seven, it'll be seven the year afterwards and if it's seven, it'll be forty-seven the year afterwards.

*1* What is surprising?
*2* Why does the audience laugh?
*3* How does this part of the extract relate to the theme of the talk?

**GROUPS OF THREE**

**1** Look at the short piece of script and do 1 and 2 below.

> The point being that throughout the economies of the industrialised world we are beset with a degree of ambiguity, uncertainty and madness never before seen.

▮ **GLOSSARY** ▮

beset with *troubled by*
ambiguity *a situation in which things have more than one meaning*

*1* Summarise the point that Peters is making in your own words.
*2* Peters emphasises his point by using a group of three words. Find the group of three in the script. Do these words have different or similar meanings?

**2** Listen to the whole of Extract 3 again. Make a note of as many groups of three words as you can. Compare your lists with others in the class. Do the words in your lists have different or similar meanings?

**3** Fill each of the gaps in these sentences with two words, to make a group of three words to emphasise the point. Compare your ideas with others in the class.

*1* My real point here is that we are facing very big _____ _____ problems.
*2* The most important thing is that we never allow this kind of terrible _____ _____ mistake to happen again.
*3* Modern companies face a world of chaos, _____ _____ .

**USING CONTRAST**

**1**   Tom Peters also emphasises his points by using contrast. Look at the script of the end of the extract and answer the questions below.

> And why that is so significant is that our organisations are designed in a perverse way to not be able to deal with that.
>
> The organisational model is the standard average chugalong Henry Ford production line model and in fact we're now required to build organisations that welcome, love and cherish ambiguity and reorganisation on a weekly basis, rather than a once a decade basis.
>
> It is a crazy time indeed.

**■ GLOSSARY ■**

perverse *deliberately wrong or unreasonable*

chugalong *old-fashioned*

1 What kind of organisation does he want to see?
2 What is that contrasted with?
3 How often does he think companies should reorganise?
4 What is that contrasted with?

**2**   Now fill the gaps in these sentences to make some contrasts. Compare your ideas with others in the class.

1 We need these products in the shops next week, not _____ .
2 We have got to stop treating our customers like _____ and start treating them like _____ .
3 Our future lies with employees who _____ , not with the ones who _____ .

**PRESENTING AND YOU**

  Each person should think of a very short (one minute) presentation to give to the rest of the group. Choose one of these subjects.

■ changes in the international business environment over the next few years
■ the future of the motor car
■ possible future changes in your company or in the area where you live

Use groups of three words, contrast, humour and surprise as appropriate. Also think about pausing and emphasis.

# issues

## *The long now*

**THE LONG NOW** 👥👥 Read the text and talk about the questions below.

*I*n the 1980s, Danny Hillis became famous as the man who built the fastest computer in the world, The Connection Machine. But in the 1990s, he decided that the computer industry suffered from having a much too short-term view of the future. He believed that business was focusing on what was for lunch instead of thinking about how to feed the world.

*So he set himself the task of building a clock that would tell the time for the next 10,000 years – the clock of the long now. Hillis believed that building the clock was more than just a practical engineering challenge. It provided an opportunity to think about the way that civilisation will evolve.*

1 Do you agree with Danny Hillis that most businesspeople are only interested in the short term? Give examples to support your argument.
2 Imagine that you were designing the clock of the long now. Talk about these questions.

▋ What kind of clock would it be?
▋ How would you power it?
▋ Where would you locate it?
▋ What kind of materials would you use?
▋ How would you make its purpose clear to future generations?

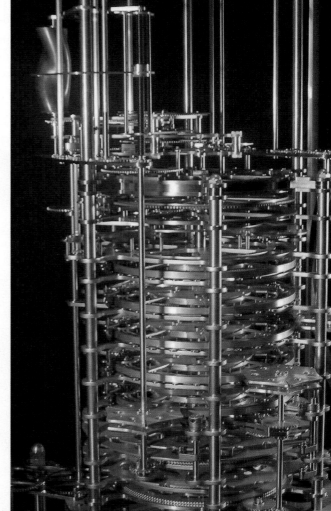

## PRESENTING YOUR VISION

Work in groups of two or four people and prepare a team presentation.

1 Think of a project that you think will still be useful in 100 years' time. (It could be a new road, a development in medicine, a hotel in space or even the rules for a new sport!)

2 Prepare a presentation for the rest of the class in which you try to persuade them to contribute money to make your vision a reality. A suggested structure is as follows:

■ Introduce the purpose and structure of your presentation.

■ Explain what problem your project aims to solve or what needs it hopes to address.

■ Describe how you plan to realise your vision and what the money will be used for.

■ Summarise and conclude.

3 Each group should take turns to give their presentation to the rest of the class, with each group member giving a different part of the presentation.

4 Discuss which presentation was the most persuasive and why.

## AND FINALLY ...

Perhaps one of the most difficult things in business is to communicate your vision clearly. Think about the problems of communication by doing this activity.

1 Everybody in the class should get a large blank piece of paper. One member of the class should act as the class leader and read out these instructions to the rest of the class, allowing time for everyone to do each step.

1 Close your eyes and fold the piece of paper in half.

2 Fold it in half again.

3 Fold it in half a third time.

4 Tear off the top left-hand corner.

5 Tear off a piece from the middle of the bottom of the paper.

6 Open your eyes, unfold the paper and hold it up for the rest of the group to see.

2 What do your patterns tell you about the difficulties of clearly communicating your vision?

# interactions

## 2 managing change

### doing business 2 *Discussing ideas*

#### BRAINSTORMING

Instead of relying on deterrents, the Dutch city authorities decided to encourage people to use the litter bins that they provided. So they designed a special type of bin that told a joke every time a piece of rubbish was pushed through its lid.

The British police decided to place bikes all over the city that could be used by anybody at no cost. When a person had finished their journey, they simply leant the bike against a wall and left it for somebody else to ride.
The idea worked well for a time but, before too long, criminals in other places heard about the 'free' bikes and visited the city very late one night with several big lorries …

## 4 face to face

### doing business 1 *Tough meetings*

#### WHAT OZWALD BOATENG DID NEXT

'Give me time to pay,' Boateng said to the receivers. They agreed to do so, and Boateng's business was soon thriving again; in 2000 he was named as British Menswear Designer of the Year.

## Role cards: Student A

## 4 face to face

### doing business 1 *Tough meetings*

#### TOUGH ROLES

**Role play 1**

You have paid **B**'s company to build a new house for you. The work is now over three months behind schedule and you and your family are running out of both money and patience!

**Role play 2**

The car that **B** sold you has already broken down three times and you have spent so much on repairs that you now can't afford to pay **B** the money that you owe.

### doing business 2 *Answering questions*

#### A + 1 ROLES

**Role play 1**

You are an engineer who wants to know why a new brick wall has fallen down at a building site.

**Role play 2**

You are a member of staff and **B** is your boss. You are often late because you miss the train, but you want to point out that you work until after 8 o'clock most evenings.

## 8 the deal

### doing business 2 *Negotiating tactics*

#### NEGOTIATING ROLES

**Role play 1**

You are a representative of a multinational company who is visiting **B**'s small software company to negotiate the purchase of some new data management software. You have been told that you can pay up to $250,000 for the software, but after-sales service must be free for at least three years.

**Role play 2**

You are trying to buy a fairly unusual secondhand sports car from **B**, but you don't want to pay more than $23,000 for it.

# 7 paranoia

## doing **business 2** *Body language*

### READING BODY LANGUAGE

Possible answers in British/American business culture:

*1* Lying  *2* Preparing to move into action  *3* Uncertainty
*4* A negative reaction  *5* Defensiveness  *6* Superiority
*7* Disapproval  *8* Approval

# 8 the **deal**

## introduction

### THREE CULTURES

Text on left: the Arab world
Text below in centre: the USA
Text on right: Japan

## Role cards: Student B

# 4 **face** to **face**

## doing **business 1** *Tough meetings*

### TOUGH ROLES

**Role play 1**

You're building a house for **A**, but the work is three months behind schedule. Your small company currently has too much work but you don't want to employ more workers because you are trying to cut costs.

**Role play 2**

You sold a car to **A**, but said that he/she didn't need to pay for it for two or three weeks. Over two months have now passed and you need the money.

## doing **business 2** *Answering questions*

### A + 1 ROLES

**Role play 1**

You are a builder and a brick wall you have just built has fallen down. You know that the wrong kind of cement was used, but you want to point out that this is the first time that something like this has happened all year.

**Role play 2**

You are a manager who wants to know why your staff are always ten minutes late in the morning.

# 8 the **deal**

## doing **business 2** *Negotiating tactics*

### NEGOTIATING ROLES

**Role play 1**

You are sales manager of a small software company. **A** is visiting your office because he/she wants to buy some data management software. You are quite happy to give the software away for nothing because the company makes its money from its after-sales service contracts, which normally make around $80,000–$100,000 per year.

**Role play 2**

You paid $25,000 just over a year ago for a sports car you're selling and you want to make a small profit on it.

# Contents

grammar reference

# 1 Articles

## Indefinite article

We use **a / an**

1 before singular countable nouns mentioned for the first time or when we are not being specific
*A fool and his money are soon parted.*

2 before professions
*She's **an** architect and he's **a** consultant.*

3 in expressions of measurement
*The price of crude oil was $15 **a** barrel.*

## Definite article

We use **the**

1 before a noun that we have mentioned before
*I had a BMW and a Porsche but I sold **the** BMW.*

2 when what we are referring to is clear from the situation
*I'll meet you at **the** station in **the** entrance hall.*

3 before adjectives or nouns that refer to a category of people or things
***the** middle classes    **the** unemployed    **the** British*
*The way that we do business has been completely changed by **the** Internet.*

4 before some institutions
***the** Stock Exchange    **the** World Bank*

5 in superlative expressions
*General Motors is **the** biggest car manufacturer in the world.*

## Zero article

We use **no article (zero article)**

1 with countable or uncountable nouns used in a general sense
*It's great to have **money** but it can't buy you **love.***
***Winners** make things happen; **losers** let things happen.*

2 after prepositions in certain fixed expressions
*at work    at home    in bed    by plane    after lunch*

3 with most countries, languages and public places
*Australia, Chile, Japanese, Russian, Buckingham Palace, Carnegie Hall*
    (But note: *the Netherlands, the Rockefeller Center, the Eiffel Tower*)

---

**PRACTICE**

**1** Complete the sentences using *a / an*, *the* or Ø (no article).

1 'What does his wife do?' 'She's _____ engineer'.

2 'How often to you come to England?' 'Three or four times _____ year'.

3 'How did you spend _____ weekend?' 'In _____ bed. I had _____ bad cold.'

4 Nothing succeeds like _____ success.

5 _____ wise do at once what _____ foolish do later.

6 _____ consumers are not stupid; they just act stupid.

7 _____ lawyer is _____ person who gets two people to undress and then runs off with their clothes.

8 '_____ woman is like _____ teabag. Only in _____ water do you realise how strong she is.' (Nancy Reagan)

**2** Complete these two newspaper articles using *a / an*, *the* or Ø (no article).

## THE DISNEY BRAND

1 _____ well-established brand name can broaden 2 _____ company's ambitions, allowing it to introduce 3 _____ new products or move into 4 _____ new markets. For example, Walt Disney has stretched its brand name well beyond 5 _____ films to cover many other services and products. People don't have to pay 30 per cent more for 6 _____ Disney T-shirt. But they do so because 7 _____ Disney name means more to them than just 8 _____ ordinary T-shirt – it embodies 9 _____ Disney magic.

## COMPUTER CONTROL

10 _____ professor of 11 _____ cybernetics has become 12 _____ first person in 13 _____ USA to have 14 _____ special silicon chip implanted in his body. 15 _____ chip allows 16 _____ department's computers to communicate directly with his body. 'As I walk around 17 _____ building, all 18 _____ lights go on, and when I scratch my head some of 19 _____ computers burst into 20 _____ life. It can be quite scary,' he said.

# 2 Conditionals (1)

## Zero, first and second conditionals

We use conditional sentences when we talk about realistic or hypothetical situations and their probable results. Something may or may not happen, depending on the circumstances.

1   The zero conditional states a general rule or truth. The verbs in both the *if* clause and the main clause are in the present tense.
    *If you **treat** people well, they usually **perform** well.*
    *You **get** coffee with sugar if you **press** this button.*

2   The first conditional talks about a realistic situation and its probable result. The verb in the *if* clause is in the present (or present perfect) and the verb in the main clause is in the future. We can use *might* or *could* if we are less certain of the result.
    *If we **raise** more capital, we**'ll be able to** invest more.*
    *If we **don't raise** more capital, we**'re going to have** problems in six months' time.*
    *If we **don't raise** more capital, we **might have** problems in six months' time.*
    *I**'ll be** furious if he **has wiped** anything off my hard drive.*

3   *If … not* can be replaced by *unless*.
    *We'll have problems **if** we **don't raise** more capital.*
    *We'll have problems **unless** we **raise** more capital.*

4   We use the second conditional for hypothetical, more tentative situations, with the verb in the *if* clause in the past simple and the verb in the main clause preceded by *would*. *Might* or *could* can also be used if we are less certain.
    *If the CEO **knew** what he was doing, the company **would be** much more secure.*
    ***Would** you **be** happier if you **were** in a different department?*
    *We **could get** there on time if the taxi driver **tried** a different route.*

5   The second conditional is also used for unreal or imaginary situations.
    *Where **would** you **go** if someone **gave** you a ticket to any destination in the world?*
    *If I **was** the CEO, I **would** soon **organise** this place properly.*

6   In the second conditional, *were* can be used instead of *was* with the first and third person singular.
    *If he **were** the CEO, we**'d have** much better conditions.*
    *If I **were** you, I**'d get** on with some work.*

## PRACTICE

**1** Match these examples to the descriptions below.

  1   If pollution continues at present levels, many trees will die.
  2   If you interrupt people, they get angry.
  3   If you went to Liverpool, where would you stay?
  4   If you went to work by helicopter, how long would it take?

  a   something that is generally true
  b   something in the future that is possible but not probable
  c   something that is unreal or imaginary
  d   something that is seen as probable in the future, given present circumstances

**2** Match the two halves of these sentences.

  1   If we don't get this contract,
  2   You can't travel on this train if
  3   If anyone asks for me,
  4   If we want to reach more customers,
  5   If you reach the target,

  a   we'll go bankrupt.
  b   we'll have to advertise more.
  c   you'll get a bonus.
  d   I'll be in the canteen.
  e   you don't have a reservation.

**3** Use these situations to make first and second conditional sentences.

  1   Perhaps I'll win first prize in this competition. Then I'll get a silver cup.
      *If I win first prize in this competition, I'll get a silver cup.*
  2   I might win the lottery (which I don't often enter). Then I'd buy a yacht and a plane.
  3   The computers aren't working today. We can't send any e-mails.
  4   My advice is to spend plenty of time preparing for the presentation.
  5   I'll never become a manager in this company. As a result, I'm going to resign and look for another job.
  6   They may arrive at 9.30 instead of 10. In that case we'll be able to start the meeting early.

# 3 Conditionals (2)

Third conditional

1  When speculating about things which did not happen in the past and the consequences if they had happened, we use the third conditional, with the past perfect in the *if* clause and *would have* and the past participle in the main clause.

*If you **had told** me earlier, I **would have acted** on the information.*

*If they **had made** the right strategic decisions, they **wouldn't have gone** bankrupt.*

2  *Might have* and *could have* are also possible when we are less certain about the possible consequences.

*The joint venture **could have succeeded** if the management styles **hadn't clashed**.*

*If the speaker **had used** some good slides, the presentation **might not have been** so boring.*

3  Mixed conditional sentences do not follow the same patterns as those above and on page 129 [Conditionals (1) in this Grammar reference]. We can use different tenses depending on the situation.

We quite often speculate on a possible present situation which depends on a past action.

*She **would** probably **be** the manager of this branch if she **had performed** better at the interview.*

(She didn't perform well – in a past situation, so she isn't the manager – now.)

*If we **had left** earlier, we **would be** there by now.*

(We didn't leave early so we aren't there now.)

A hypothetical (second conditional) situation can affect what happens or doesn't happen in the past or present.

*If I **thought** she was a liar, I **wouldn't have put** her in a position of trust.*

(I don't think she is a liar, so I put her in a position of trust.)

*If Jane **wasn't** so slow she **could have finished** hours ago.*

(She is always slow, which explains why she hasn't finished.)

Punctuation: in conditional sentences, we use a comma after the *if* clause when it precedes the main clause; we don't use a comma if the main clause comes before the *if* clause.

## PRACTICE

**1**  Look at the following pairs of sentences and answer the questions.

1  If he hadn't taken out such a big loan, he wouldn't be so short of money now.
   a  Did he take out a big loan?
   b  Is he short of money?

2  If he had taken out a big loan, he would be short of money now.
   a  Did he take out a big loan?
   b  Is he short of money?

3  If she weren't on holiday, she would have been able to see her daughter.
   a  Is she on holiday?
   b  Did she see her daughter?

4  If she had been on holiday, she wouldn't have been able to see her daughter.
   a  Is she on holiday?
   b  Did she see her daughter?

**2**  Use the appropriate form of the verbs in brackets to make third conditional sentences.

1  If he (not drive) so fast, he (not skid) on the icy road.

2  We (make) an absolute fortune if there (not be) such a major change in the tax laws.

3  They (spend) all day surfing the Internet if the boss (stay) at the conference.

4  What (happen) if the government (take) a different attitude towards the euro?

5  If the company (not invest) overseas, the workers here (keep) their jobs.

**3**  Complete the two possible endings to these situations with the appropriate form of the verbs in brackets.

1  If I hadn't let my daughter borrow the car,
   a  I _____ to lend it to you today.
   b  she _____ to get to her interview last week.
      (be able/not be able)

2  If I had taken on a replacement secretary,
   a  I _____ out this report now.
   b  I _____ myself a lot of time and effort.
      (not type/save)

3  If the finance minister had been a little more competent,
   a  the stock market _____ a nosedive.
   b  the country _____ in a better economic situation than it is at present.    (not take/be)

# 4 Future (1)

1  We use the present continuous to talk about plans and future arrangements.
*I'm **meeting** Mrs Venuti next week. She's **arriving** on Thursday and she's **staying** at the Grand Hotel.*
*What **are you doing** at the weekend?*

2  We use *going to* to talk about plans, decisions and present intentions for the future.
*He says he is **going to** ask for promotion.*
  (= he's decided to)
*What are you **going to** say at the board meeting?*
  (= what do you intend to say?)

3  We also use *going to* to make a short-term prediction when there is external evidence for a future event.
*The market seems to indicate that the share price is **going to** fall even further.*

4  We use *will* for longer-term predictions.
*This company **will** be in the top 100 companies in five years' time.*

5  We also prefer *will* when we state our own ideas and judgement.
*I guess she'**ll** be extremely angry when she hears the news.*

6  We use *will* when making a spontaneous promise or offer.
*I'**ll** have the report on your desk first thing tomorrow.*
*Don't worry about transport. We'**ll** ring for a taxi.*

7  We use the present simple to refer to a future event based on an official calendar or schedule.
*The train **leaves** from Warsaw at 12.24.*
*The next planning meeting **is** on 3 March.*

8  We use the present simple or the present perfect in clauses beginning with *when, before, after, as soon as* and *until* to refer to future time.
*Give me a ring <u>when</u> you **arrive**.*
*I'll send you an email <u>as soon as</u> I **get** the results.*
*I'll let you know <u>after</u> I'**ve spoken** to the boss.*

## PRACTICE

1  Match the grammar rules to the examples below.

 1  We use this form to express present intentions for the future.

 2  We use this form to express a decision made at the moment of speaking.

 3  This form is used to make predictions based on external evidence.

 4  We use this form to refer to timetabled events.

 5  We use this form to talk about arrangements for the future made before the moment of speaking.

 a  Don't get up. I'll answer it.

 b  Next year is going to be our best year ever.

 c  I'm having lunch with her on Friday.

 d  The 8.30 train gets in at 9.05.

 e  I'm going to learn Spanish.

2  Caroline is planning to visit Russia soon and is talking to her colleague. Read the dialogue and decide which of the sentences is more appropriate each time.

 1  CAROLINE
   a  I will go to Moscow soon.
   b  I'm going to Moscow soon.

 2  TERRI
   a  What are you doing in Moscow?
   b  What do you do in Moscow?

 3  CAROLINE
   a  I'm meeting Natasha Grigorian.
   b  I meet Natasha Grigorian.

 4  TERRI
   a  When are you leaving?
   b  When will you leave?

 5  CAROLINE
   a  On Tuesday. I'm giving you a call when I arrive.
   b  On Tuesday. I'll give you a call when I arrive.

# 5 Future (2)

1  We use the future continuous to talk about events which will be in progress at a particular point in the future.

   *I'll be compiling the statistics during the week and should have them ready by Friday.*

   *He's due to retire soon and I expect that this time next year he'll be writing his memoirs.*

2  If the event will be completed before a particular point in the future, we use the future perfect.

   *I'll have finished the work before the end of May.*

   *We'll have spent $10 million on research and development by the time the product is finally launched.*

3  If we want to emphasise how long something has been going on at a particular point in the future, we use the future perfect continuous.

   *By February next year she'll have been working for the same company for 25 years.*

4  We use *be* + infinitive to make official announcements. This form is often seen in the press.

   *The Prime Minister is to visit Moscow next week.*

   *The two companies are to hold talks in the autumn with a view to a merger.*

   In newspaper headlines the verb *to be* is omitted.

# PM TO VISIT MOSCOW

5  We often use *be* + infinitive in sentences beginning with *if* to say that one thing must happen before something else can happen.

   *If we are to become a truly global company, we must be present in every market.*

**1**  In which sentence, *1* or *2*, is the speaker referring to something that will have started before they get to Moscow?

   1  When we get to Moscow, I guess it will snow.

   2  When we get to Moscow, I guess it will be snowing.

**2**  Complete these sentences with the most appropriate endings.

   1  I expect I'll work at Matra for about three years

   2  I will have been working at Matra for about three years

   3  I'll be interviewing the candidates

   4  I'll interview the candidates

   a  ... and then I'll call you.

   b  ... and then look for something else.

   c  ... so please don't call.

   d  ... before I have any chance of being promoted.

**3**  Match these questions to the appropriate replies.

   1  Will you help me with the arrangements?

   2  Will you be helping me with the arrangements?

   a  Yes, if you like.

   b  Yes, I think so.

**4**  Complete these sentences using the future continuous, future perfect or an infinitive future.

   1  By 2050, the Netherlands (disappear) under water.

   2  In the the 22nd century, we (use) telepathy to communicate with each other.

   3  The PM has just announced that the government (introduce) new legislation by the end of the year.

   4  By 2025, Mandarin Chinese (become) the international language of business.

   5  From about 2015, many parents (choose) the colour of their children's skin.

   6  With a bit of luck, this time next year we (launch) the new Internet software and the money (roll) in.

# 6 Infinitive and gerund (1)

1   There are various forms of the infinitive, in both the active and passive.

|  | ACTIVE | PASSIVE |
|---|---|---|
| Present | *to do* | *to be done* |
| Present continuous | *to be doing* | – |
| Past | *to have done* | *to have been done* |
| Past continuous | *to have been doing* | – |

The continuous form is rarely used in the passive. For negative infinitives we use *not* before the *to*.

2   When verbs are followed by another verb, it can often be difficult to know whether the second verb should be in the infinitive or should end in *-ing*. However, it can be useful to group verbs according to meaning, as verbs of similar meaning tend to be followed by one or the other form.

The infinitive (with *to*) is used after the verbs in the following categories:
communication: *ask, claim, decline, offer, persuade, promise, request, say, tell, warn*
desire: *hope, prefer, regret, want, wish*
intention: *agree, aim, choose, decide, intend, mean, plan, refuse, threaten*
effort: *attempt, fail, manage, seek, struggle, try*
causation: *allow, arrange, enable, encourage, instruct, tempt*
thought: *expect, believe, consider, forget, pretend, remind*

Similarly, the *-ing* form is used after the verbs in these categories:
progression: *go on, keep (on), spend (time), start*
communication: *complain about, mention, propose, recommend, suggest, talk about*
thought: *believe in, concentrate on, consider, forget about, recall, think about*
attitude: *count on, deplore, detest, dread, enjoy, feel like, mind, prefer, resent*
accusation/apology: *admit (to), apologise for, confess to, deny, justify*

## PRACTICE

**1** Complete the sentences using a verb in the infinitive or gerund so that the new sentence has a similar meaning to the original one.

1   I'm sorry I was late.
    I apologise …

2   She anticipates getting a positive response soon.
    She expects …

3   They're saying that they will change supplier if we increase our prices.
    They are threatening …

4   She says she has the chairman's confidence.
    She claims …

5   I think we should try again.
    I recommend …

6   It wasn't his intention to be rude.
    He didn't wish …

7   Hard work doesn't bother me as long as I'm not under too much pressure.
    I don't mind …

8   In my job I make difficult decisions all the time.
    My job involves …

9   I would very much like to see you soon.
    I hope …

10   Going into work has become a nightmare for her.
    She dreads …

11   He said he was not going to comment.
    He refused …

12   How on earth could you spend so much on entertainment?
    How can you justify …

**2** Reorder the words to make correct sentences.

1   job was encouraged the apply he to for

2   chief they resign are the executive to expecting

3   work she instructed for at to was report 8 o'clock

4   he her from complaint prevent can't making a

5   the Bank poor for enables borrow countries development money projects World to

6   to they were targets they but lying reached claimed their have

# 7 *Infinitive and gerund (2)*

*1* Some verbs are followed by either the infinitive or the *-ing* form with little change in meaning.
*They don't **like working** at weekends.*
*They don't **like to work** at weekends.*

However, the use of the infinitive or gerund with the following verbs does alter the meaning.
*I will never **forget** meeting Bill Clinton.*
    (= I will always remember.)
*I often **forget** to switch off my computer.*
    (= I fail to remember.)

*He **remembers** locking the safe.*
    (= He has a clear memory of this.)
*He **remembered** to lock the safe.*
    (= He didn't forget.)

*If I got promotion, it would **mean** moving.*
    (= involve)
*I didn't **mean** to be rude.*
    (= intend to)

*She was an alcoholic but **stopped** drinking.*
    (= didn't do it any more)
*She **stopped** to have a drink on the way back home.*
    (= interrupted something in order to)

*If you get stressed, **try** taking long, deep breaths.*
    (= experiment and see what happens)
*She **tried** to learn Japanese but gave up.*
    (= attempted/made the effort)

*She graduated in law and **went on** to become mayor of New York.*
    (= what she did next)
*I put the receiver down but the phone **went on** ringing.*
    (= continued)

*2* Many adjectives are followed by an infinitive. They fall into a number of categories.
<u>likelihood</u>: *certain, likely, unlikely, sure*
<u>willingness</u>: *determined, eager, reluctant*
<u>emotion</u>: *afraid, glad, sorry, surprised*
<u>evaluation</u>: *convenient, right, useless*
<u>importance</u>: *essential, important, vital*
<u>degree of difficulty</u>: *complicated, easy, hard*

*3* We can also use the infinitive after certain nouns.
*It's a good **idea to start** meetings on time.*
*She was a complete **idiot to agree**.*
*It's a **pleasure to see** you again.*
*It would be a **shame to give up** now.*

**1** Choose the correct form of the verb in Italics.

1 Damn! I've forgotten *to bring/bringing* my briefcase.

2 I'll never forget *to be/being* made redundant for the first time.

3 I'll always remember *to meet/meeting* such a big star – it was a wonderful experience.

4 Remember *to switch/switching* off the computer before you leave.

5 If I went to live in the States, it would mean *to leave/leaving* my wife and family behind.

6 Sorry, I didn't mean *to sound/sounding* angry.

7 If you would only stop *to talk/talking* and try *to listen/listening* for once!

8 After two hours at the computer, she stopped *to have/having* a cup of coffee.

9 If your back hurts at the end of the day, try *to do/doing* some simple stretching exercises.

10 Don't get impatient – he's only trying *to help/helping*.

11 After a successful career in television, she went on *to become/becoming* a successful businesswoman.

12 He just went on *to talk/talking* and didn't listen to me at all.

**2** Join the two halves of the sentences with one of the adjectives in the middle.

1 For the experiment to be valid, it is

2 If you haven't got much money, it can be

3 As a start-up company in a competitive area, it is

4 Given the state of the traffic, we were

5 I am very

| advantageous | essential | right | sorry | unlikely |
| --- | --- | --- | --- | --- |

a not to go by car

b to pay by monthly instalments

c to inform you that your services will no longer be required.

d to make a profit in the short term

e to record the data accurately

# 8  *Modals and related verbs (1)*

Modals and related verbs can be used with reference to actions and events that we can control: permission, obligation, advice, suggestion, prohibition.

1 To ask for or to give permission, we use *can, may* or *could*.
**Can** I use your mobile phone?
'**May** I see what's in the report?'
'No, I'm afraid you **can't**. It's confidential.'

2 To indicate obligation, we use *must* or *have to*.
Protective clothing **must** be worn.
I **have to** change trains twice to get to work.

If something was necessary or obligatory in the past, we use *had to*, and in the future *will have to*.
When we lived in Mexico, we **had to** learn some Spanish.
We **will have to** look at the revised figures next month.

3 When we impose the obligation on ourselves, we tend to use *must,* and *have to* when the obligation is imposed by others or by external circumstances.
I really **must** remember to phone him.
We **have to** be at our desks by 9 o'clock in the morning.

4 The absence of obligation is expressed by *don't have to.*
She works from home so she **doesn't have to** commute.

5 For advice and suggestions we use *should* and *ought to.*
Do you think we **ought to** reconsider our investments?
You really **should** relax after a hard day at the office.

6 To express the idea that something is prohibited, we use *must not* or *cannot.*
Passengers **must not** use their mobile phones on the plane.
You **cannot** import goods without a licence.

7 If we have present evidence with which to make a deduction, we use *must* or *can't.*
You **must** be very tired after such a long journey.
That **can't** be Mrs Taylor at reception – she's in Cracow.

To make deductions about the past, we use *must have* or *can't have.*
Their journey home **must have** been awful: they were stuck on the runway for eight hours.
She **can't have** forgotten – I got her to repeat the instruction three times.

If we are less sure of our deduction, we use *could, may* or *might.*
I haven't seen him around – he **could have** gone to the seminar, or I suppose he **might have** gone home early.

## PRACTICE

Match the signs to the following sentences and complete each one by choosing the appropriate modal verb.

1 You *don't have to / mustn't* pay to go in.
2 You *can / should* phone from here.
3 All valuables *can / cannot* be put in the safe.
4 Masks *must / can* be worn.
5 You *should / may* always wear a safety belt.
6 You *must not / do not have to* enter these premises.
7 You *don't have to / must not* pay.
8 You *must not / do not have to* exceed the speed limit.
9 You *will have to / don't have to* pay to get your car back.
10 You *must not / will have to* overtake.
11 You *can't / can* park here unless you are disabled.
12 Hardhats *must / could* be worn.
13 You *cannot / should* lock it when you leave it.
14 You *shouldn't / ought to* shut down your computer when not in use.

135

# 9  *Modals and related verbs (2)*

Modals can be used with reference to events or states of likelihood that we can't control.

1 With reference to possibility, we use *can* to say that something is possible and *cannot* if something is impossible.
*Travel* **can** *be really boring.*
*You* **can't** *judge a book by looking at its cover.*

If a situation is possible but it is not certain that it will happen, we use *could, may* or *might.* (*May* suggests that something is more likely than *might.*)
*If we downsized, we* **could** *save a lot of money.*
*I think you should give it a try – you* **may/might** *find it's not so bad after all.*

We also use *could* if we want to say something was possible in the past.
*Many years ago you* **could** *drive a car without taking a test.*

2 Past opportunities which were missed are expressed using *could have* or *might have* and a past participle.
*She* **could have risen** *to the top if she had had any ambition.*
*She* **might have found** *it easier to get on if she'd been more approachable.*

3 The following is a guide to how certain we feel when we use different modals.

| | |
|---|---|
| 100% certain | *He* **will** *be there by now.* |
| very certain | *He* **should** *be there by now.* |
| pretty certain | *He* **may/could** *well be there by now.* |
| not very certain | *He* **may/might** *be there by now.* |
| impossible | *He* **can't/won't** *be there by now.* |

**1** Choose the best way to complete each sentence.

1 Living and working abroad
  a can be enriching but also stressful.
  b can't be enriching but also stressful.
  c can't have been enriching but also stressful.

2 They phoned to say they were on their way an hour ago, so I think
  a they should have got lost.
  b they had to have got lost.
  c they must have got lost.

3 The firm has been taken over by an American conglomerate so
  a she could have learnt English fast.
  b she will have to learn English fast.
  c she might have learnt English fast.

4 Everything is running OK so
  a you shouldn't have too much trouble.
  b you shouldn't have had too much trouble.
  c you may have too much trouble.

5 She can't have left already!
  a She will be there by now.
  b It must be 6 o'clock.
  c She only arrived 5 minutes ago.

6 They should be there by now –
  a they left hours ago.
  b they mustn't have got lost.
  c they could have arrived.

**2** Match the sentence halves.

1 It's a good idea to invest in a company which is about to be taken over – you

2 Why didn't you follow up your application? You

3 He should have stayed in the States – he

4 You must try to do your best at the interview – you

a might have got a job offer.

b could make a lot of money.

c might get a job offer.

d could have made a lot of money.

# 10 *Nouns*

*1* Most nouns are **countable** and have a singular and plural form.

*He's **a good worker** and he gets on well with all the other **workers** here.*

*2* Some nouns are always **uncountable**. This means that they do not have a plural form, they are used with a singular verb and they are not preceded by *a / an*.

Here are some common uncountable nouns which are often countable in other languages:

| | | | |
|---|---|---|---|
| *accommodation* | *advertising* | *advice* | *baggage* |
| *cash* | *damage* | *employment* | *equipment* |
| *furniture* | *hardware* | *information* | *insurance* |
| *legislation* | *merchandise* | *money* | *news* |
| *progress* | *research* | *shopping* | *software* |
| *transport* | *traffic* | *training* | *travel* |
| *weather* | *work* | | |

*3* Some nouns have countable **C** and uncountable **U** uses.

*He doesn't have much **experience** of computer **programming**.* **U**

*Living in Vietnam was **an interesting experience**.* **C**

*She dislikes her **work**.* **U**

*If you take the back off this clock you can see the **works** inside.* **C**

*4* Uncountable nouns can usually be made countable by using another expression.

| |
|---|
| *advice / a piece of advice    insurance / an insurance policy    money / a coin / a banknote / a sum news / an item of news    training / a training course* |

*5* Plural nouns only have a plural form, they cannot be used with *a / an* and they usually take a plural verb form.

| | | | |
|---|---|---|---|
| *clothes* | *goods* | *earnings* | *outskirts* |
| *headquarters* | *jeans* | *premises* | *valuables* |

*6* Compound nouns are formed by putting two or more nouns together. They are sometimes written as one word and sometimes as two words – with or without a hyphen.

| | | | |
|---|---|---|---|
| *powerhouse* | *workplace* | *headhunter* | *website* |
| *bank account* | *law court* | *phone card* | |
| *web camera* | *video-conferencing* | | |

---

**PRACTICE**

**1** Match each uncountable noun on the left with a plural countable noun that is related to it in meaning.

| | |
|---|---|
| advertising | trips |
| traffic | machines |
| equipment | commercials |
| insurance | suggestions |
| employment | laws |
| travel | bulletins |
| progress | jobs |
| advice | vehicles |
| legislation | policies |
| news | advances |

**2** Choose the correct form in each of the following sentences.

*1* We've placed *an advertisement/advertising* in the local newspaper.

*2* I always use *a public transport/public transport* because of *a heavy traffic/heavy traffic* at rush hour.

*3* Could you give me *an advice/some advice*?

*4* I've bought *a software/some software* to help me design my web page.

*5* She works from *a home/home* as *a headhunter/ headhunter*.

**3** The text below was written to help managers in UK companies to operate internationally. Complete the text using these compound nouns.

| | |
|---|---|
| sales leads | exhibition staff |
| exhibition stand | display materials |
| publicity campaign | translation agency |

If you are planning a ¹_____ in a non-English speaking market, or are just setting up an ²_____ , you will need more than a few days' language training.

Your requirements would be to make sure that your ³_____ , brochures and pamphlets are written in the local language by a reputable ⁴_____ and that your ⁵_____ are fully able to speak directly to customers in their own language and follow up any ⁶_____ .

## 11 *Passive*

*1* The passive is formed by using the appropriate tense of the verb *to be* plus the past participle of the verb:
*(to) be done, is/are done, will be done, was/were done, have/has been done, had been done,* etc.

*2* We use a passive structure when we do not focus on who performs an action, or it is not necessary to know.
*The application **was refused**.*
*The new installation **is being built**.*
*He **has been asked** to go to Singapore.*
*He likes **to be congratulated** when he's done well.*

*3* If we also want to say who performs the action, we can use the passive and a phrase beginning with *by*.
*The application **was refused** by the planning committee.*
*The new installation **is being built** by a German firm.*
*He **has been asked** by his boss to go to Singapore.*

*4* We use the passive to describe things like processes because we are more concerned with the process itself than with who carries it out.

### THE RECYCLING OF CANS

Aluminium cans **are taken** to collection centres where they **are crushed**. They are then **transported** to special plants in order to **be recycled**. The cans have to **be put** into a furnace so that they can **be melted** in the intense heat. Once they **have been removed** from the furnace, they **are shaped** into rectangular bars, weighing at least 10,000 kg.

*5* In a formal style of writing (e.g. the minutes of a meeting, reports, etc.) we often choose an impersonal style by beginning sentences with *It* followed by a passive verb form.
*It **has been suggested** that we should use the services of a headhunter.*
*It **was thought** to be an attractive option.*
*It is now **felt** that the sums allocated were insufficient.*

---

### PRACTICE

Complete this flowchart using either passive or active verbs in the appropriate form.

#### Setting up an information system

*Clarifying outcomes*
What the system is to achieve must (clarify)[1] by both the designer and the end-user.

*Undertaking a feasibility study*
Before starting any large-scale work, an examination must (make)[2] to determine whether or not the desired outcomes can (achieve)[3].

*Obtaining approval*
All information systems cost money, and therefore the agreement of senior management should (obtain)[4] at the outset of the project.

*Research and analysis*
At this stage, relevant data (collect)[5] and (analyse)[6] in order to establish who (do)[7] what, when, how often, and so on.

*Designing and testing the new system*
A sequence of activities or processes (map out)[8] in order to systematise aspects such as the type of data to (collect)[9] and how to store and access it.

Prior to its implementation, the new system should (test)[10] thoroughly in order to eliminate any bugs or design defects.

*Providing documentation*
Clear instructions need to (provide)[11] for all users in the form of an instruction manual for the use of all those who will (involve)[12] in using the system.

*Monitoring*
Once the system (install)[13] care must (take)[14] to ensure that it (check)[15] regularly for positive or negative feedback.

# 12 *Past simple and present perfect*

## Past simple

1 We use the past simple to talk about events or states in the past which are over. There is an interval between the time the event took place and the time we are speaking or writing about it.

*One day, Ola Pehrson **decided** to place sensors on the leaves of her yucca plant. A computer program **translated** the electrical activity into financial decisions. It **made** a healthy 18% return on investment.*

2 We often use time expressions such as *on Monday, last year, in 1997*, etc. to draw attention to the time things happened.

*Attila the Hun lived **in the fifth century.***

## Present perfect

1 The present perfect is set in indefinite time – in other words there is no precise time reference. Time expressions referring to a definite time in the past are not used.

*She's **had** several jobs abroad.*
*I've **seen** the latest figures.*

2 We use the present perfect to say that something started to happen in the past, has continued to happen up until now and is still happening.

*She **has lived** in Helsinki for many years. (She still lives there.)*
*Evelyn **has worked** for us since 1999. (and still does)*

3 We also use the present perfect to talk about something that happened in the past and is finished but still affects the present circumstances.

*The taxi **has arrived.** (It is here now.)*
*He's **lost** his wallet. (He can't find it.)*

4 Time words such as *so far, up until now, yet* and *ever* which refer to 'time up to now' occur with the present perfect.

*Have you **ever** eaten sushi?*
***So far** we haven't managed to stop computer crime very effectively.*
*A leader gets his people from where they are to where they have not **yet** been.*

5 We use *just* to show that an event has happened very recently.

*After months of struggle, the company **has just gone** into liquidation.*

---

**PRACTICE**

Complete the following passage, using either the past simple or the present perfect.

Fatboy Slim – alias Norman Cook – is a multi-millionaire who (be)[1] successful over the last few years in a number of different genres and under various pseudonyms. In the late 1980s, he (play)[2] with a group called The Housemartins before founding Beats International and then Freakpower.

Shortly after a number one hit with a jeans commercial, Norman (change)[3] into Fatboy Slim, the name which so far (make)[4] him the most money. The album *You've Come a Long Way, Baby* (sell)[5] millions of copies worldwide. And yet it (cost)[6] him almost nothing to make: he only had to pay for the DATs he (master)[7] it on, and the coffee he (drink)[8] and the cigarettes he (smoke)[9] while making it.

But there (be)[10] legal and commercial problems throughout his career. As much of his music is based on samples of other people's works, he (have to)[11] pay a lot to get copyright permission, though on occasion he (try)[12] to get away with not paying. For example, in 1995 he (use)[13] part of someone else's music on his debut album *Better Living Through Chemistry*, with the result that lawyers (argue)[14] about it for months before they (reach)[15] an out-of-court settlement. If Fatboy had asked for permission earlier, he would probably have obtained it for a few thousand dollars. But he (not do)[16] so, and the original author (receive)[17] a large sum and an ongoing royalty.

But since then, Fatboy probably (not lose)[18] too much sleep over it as he can earn £20,000 a night as a DJ. It will be interesting to see how long Cook remains as Fatboy Slim before moving on to a different genre and a new name.

# 13 *Past simple, past continuous and* used to

## Past simple

For an explanation of uses of the past simple see page 139.

## Past simple and Past continuous

We use the past continuous to describe an event in progress at a certain time in the past when another event took place. This other event is in the past simple.

*The car **broke down** while I **was driving** along the motorway.*
*We **were talking** about her when she **came** into the room.*

## Past continuous

*1* The past continuous emphasises the duration or continuity of a past event.
   *He **was working** in his office all day long.*
   *Through the whole of the 1960s, living standards in the West **were rising** rapidly.*

*2* The past continuous is used for repeated events.
   *He **was visiting** suppliers all last week so he didn't come into the office.*
   *A year ago we **were having** a lot of trouble with quality control.*

## used to

*Used to* refers to past situations that continued for a period of time but have now ceased.
*They **used to work** at Rover but they're unemployed now.*
*We **used to have** a lot of trouble with quality control but the new boss has sorted things out.*
*What **did** she **use to do** in her old job?*
*He **didn't use to like** working flexitime, but he can see the advantages now.*

---

**PRACTICE**

**1** Complete the dialogues with either the past simple or the past continuous, using the verbs in brackets.

A: I (ring)[1] your office yesterday afternoon at about 5 o'clock, but no one (answer)[2].

B: That's not surprising. All the staff (stand)[3] outside in the rain because of a bomb alert. We (not go)[4] back into the building until after 6.

C: Good afternoon, TI Cox Ltd. Can I help you?

D: Yes, I (talk)[5] to Mr Sutcliffe a moment ago and we (get)[6] cut off.

C: Sorry. I'll put you back through to his office.

E: How (you get)[7] your present job?

F: Actually, I (work)[8] in San Francisco at the time and I (meet)[9] a Dutchman who (visit)[10] California and we (start)[11] talking. I (not look)[12] for another job but he (make)[13] me an offer I couldn't refuse so I (come)[14] to Amsterdam and I've been here ever since.

**2** Robert Dale had a bad day at the office yesterday. Use the prompts to write sentences about what happened, as in the example.

walk to work/start raining

*He was walking to work when it started raining.*

*1* have meeting/be power cut

*2* computer crash/write e-mails

*3* have lunch/spill soup

*4* surf Web/computer get virus

*5* give presentation/have heart attack

**3** Underline the correct form of the verbs in these sentences.

*1* British businessmen *were wearing/used to wear* bowler hats, but now they're only for circus clowns.

*2* Last night I *dreamt/used to dream* about that awful woman who *was being/used to be* my boss.

*3* She *was driving/used to drive* a Porsche before she *went/was going* bankrupt.

*4* What *were you talking/did you use to talk* to that woman about last night? You *were being/were* on the phone for ages!

*5* He *was being/used to be* a salesman, but he *left/used to leave* because he didn't earn enough.

# 14  *Phrasal verbs*

Phrasal verbs are combinations of ordinary verbs such as *come, go, get* and a particle (an adverb or preposition) such as *down, in, on*, etc.

The most common verbs that combine with particles to make phrasal verbs are:
*take   get   put   come   go*

The most common particles are:
*up   out   on   in   off   down*

There are four main types.

1  Some phrasal verbs don't take an object.
   *What is **going on**?*
   *If the dispute continues, the government will have to **step in**.*

2  Other phrasal verbs take an object. Some of them are separable, which means that a noun can be placed either after the phrasal verb or between the verb and particle.
   *They've **turned on** the heating.*
   *They've **turned** the heating **on**.*

   However, the particle cannot be used before a pronoun.
   *They've **turned** it **on**.*
   (NOT *They've turned on it.*)

   If the noun phrase is long, it is very unusual to separate the verb and particle, especially in written English.
   *We've **stepped up** production of the new model.*
   (NOT *We've stepped production of the new model up.*)

3  Other phrasal verbs which take an object are inseparable: the verb and particle cannot be separated by an object, whether it is a pronoun or a noun.
   *Have you **asked for** permission?*
   (NOT *Have you asked permission for?*)

   *I've never **thought about** it.*
   (NOT *I've never thought it about.*)

4  Some phrasal verbs are followed by two particles. With these, we cannot place an object between the verb and particle or between the two particles.
   *I can't **get out of** the meeting.*
   *Stock options have **come in for** a lot of criticism.*
   *She's **looking forward to** it.*

## PRACTICE

**1** Tick (✓) the following sentences if they are grammatically acceptable and put a cross (✗) next to them if they are not. Then correct the unacceptable sentences.

   1  In January 2000, Bill Gates decided to step down as CEO of Microsoft.
   2  What time did you get this morning in?
   3  Did you remember to turn the light off?
   4  Did you remember to turn off it?
   5  She's looking the problem into.
   6  We carried a full investigation out.
   7  I came a very interesting article across.
   8  The government's policies have come in for a lot of criticism.
   9  How does she put up the noise with?
   10  I'm looking forward to the weekend.

**2** Which of these sentences do not need an object to complete them? Choose an appropriate ending from those given below for the sentences which do need an object.

   1  I had no idea what was going on
   2  Could you please turn down
   3  Step inside
   4  I don't know how we're going to get out of
   5  You'll need to ask for
   6  I'd like you to think about
   7  We didn't go out
   8  I wonder when the missing file will turn up
   9  I don't understand what she's getting at
   10  She has come in for

   *a*  the volume   *b*  a lot of abuse   *c*  permission
   *d*  this mess   *e*  the idea

**3** Match the verbs on the left to the phrasal verbs with a similar meaning.

   1  hire           *a*  come out
   2  recover from   *b*  get over
   3  postpone       *c*  go over
   4  emerge         *d*  put off
   5  review         *e*  take on

# 15 *Present perfect simple and present perfect continuous*

1 We use the present perfect to talk about the present results of past or recent events. The simple form tends to emphasise the result of an action, whereas the continuous form emphasises the action itself or its duration.
   *She's **lived** in this part of Berlin for three years.*
      (a simple statement of fact)
   *She's **been living** in this part of Berlin for three years.*
      (a statement which emphasises the length of time she has been in Berlin)

2 The simple form is generally used rather than the continuous for a single finished action that is relevant in the present.
   ***Have** you **heard** the news? The chairman's just **resigned**.*
   *They **have changed** their logo.*
   *The government **has announced** an increase in corporation tax.*

3 We only use the simple form with *yet, still* and *already*.
   *I've **already done** the filing but I **haven't checked** the e-mails **yet** – and I **still haven't called** the suppliers!*

4 Only the simple form can be used if the verb relates to the number of times something has been done.
   *The sales team **have made twenty** contacts this morning.*

5 We use the present perfect continuous when the focus is on an extended period of time. The situation started in the past and has not yet reached completion.
   *Stock market prices **have been rising** steadily over the past year.*
   *House prices **have been increasing** faster than the rate of inflation.*

   The above situations are incomplete; the present perfect simple, on the other hand, tells us that the action has reached an end-point.
   Compare:
   *I've **been looking** through the accounts.*
      (The focus is on the activity.)
   *I've **looked** through the accounts.*
      (The activity is complete.)

6 The continuous form is generally used to talk about the present results of a recently completed action.
   *'Why are your hands so dirty?' 'I've **been trying** to repair the photocopier.'*

## PRACTICE

Complete the gaps with the present perfect simple or continuous form of the verb. There may be more than one possible answer.

1 They've (try) for over ten years to find a cure and they still (not find) the answer.

2 Andrew's doing his best to give up but he (smoke) three cigarettes since 9 o'clock!

3 Is there no one in her office? The phone (ring) all morning.

4 She really is quite amazing and it seems she (do) everything: she (work) as a top model, she (organise) campaigns for charity, she (be) CEO of a successful business, and in the last few months she (direct) a film which should be on the cinema screens by the end of the year.

5 'Why does Robert look so pleased?'
   'The boss (give) him a rise.'

6 I (read) a book on Tax Law but it's boring and I don't think I'll finish it.

7 'You look tired.'
   'Yeah, I (drive) all day and there was an accident on the motorway.'

8 'I'm worried about Bill. He (behave) strangely recently.'
   'Why? What (he do)?'
   'Well, he (talk) to himself and (pace) up and down his office. And I (see) him making paper aeroplanes.'
   '(you talk) to him?'
   'Not yet. Do you think I should?'

9 This must be one of the most difficult things I (work) on in my life. I (look) for a solution all week without any luck at all.

10 'How much of the manual (you read) so far?'
   'About thirty pages. What (you do) all this time?'
   'Me? I (have) three cups of coffee and I (make) five phone calls – all to my girlfriend!'

## 16 *Present simple and present continuous*

### Present simple

*1* We use the present simple to give factual information.
*Our firm **employs** over 800 people and **offers** a wide range of financial services.*

*2* We use the present simple to talk about routines and say how often we do things.
*Most commuters **leave** for work at about 8 and **get** home at 6.*
*I often **speak** English at work.*
*He never **takes** work home at the weekend.*

*3* We also use the present simple to describe things which are generally true.
*Managers **need to** motivate employees.*
*People with low self-esteem **lack** confidence in their abilities.*

*4* Some verbs are normally used only in the simple form. These include verbs of:
<u>thought</u> e.g. *believe, doubt, forget, know, realise, regret, remember, suppose, think, understand*
<u>emotion</u> e.g. *admire, dislike, hate, like, love, want, wish*
<u>perception</u> e.g. *appear, be, recognise, seem, sound*
<u>possession</u> e.g. *belong to, contain, have, include, own, possess*

### Present continuous

*1* We use the present continuous to talk about an event at the moment of speaking.
*Someone **is knocking** at the door.*

*2* We also use the present continuous to talk about ongoing activities, and temporary and changing situations.
*She's **having** business English classes.*
*I'm still **writing** the report.*
*He's **living** with his mother because he's just got divorced.*
*The use of the Internet **is growing** rapidly.*

*3* The present continuous is used to emphasise that something happens repeatedly, often something that we dislike.
*He's constantly **interrupting**.*
*I'm always **forgetting** to take my keys.*

(For more on the present simple and present continuous for the future, see page 131.)

### PRACTICE

Alan is a stockbroker in the City of London. He has gone to see his doctor about his state of health.

Complete the dialogue with the present simple or present continuous, using the verb in brackets. There may be more than one possible answer.

DOCTOR: What do you think (make)[1] you feel like this now?

ALAN: Well, I'm a stockbroker and I (work)[2] for a major investment bank in the City. The pressure of work is terrible. Usually I (do)[3] about 45 hours a week but at the moment I (do)[4] over 60. At the end of each day I (take)[5] work back home with me.

DOCTOR: Yes, you (appear)[6] to be overworking. How many hours a night (you/sleep)[7] as a general rule?

ALAN: I can survive on seven hours a night but at the moment I (not sleep)[8] very well at all. So I (be)[9] perpetually tired and I can't concentrate.

DOCTOR: And I (suppose)[10] you feel the work (get)[11] on top of you and that you can't cope.

ALAN: That's right. And I'm afraid I (drink)[12] a lot as well.

DOCTOR: What is 'a lot'?

ALAN: I (have)[13] a bottle of wine every evening.

DOCTOR: By yourself?

ALAN: Yes. I (live)[14] alone. Always have done. And another thing. I (weigh)[15] myself every morning and I (think)[16] I (lose)[17] a lot of weight. And my hair (begin)[18] to fall out as well.

DOCTOR: Well, that may be normal. After all, you (not get)[19] any younger!

ALAN: No, I (understand)[20] that but I (hate)[21] the idea.

DOCTOR: But the weight loss (worry)[22] me. You (need)[23] to make sure that you (eat)[24] regularly and (have)[25] a balanced diet. I (recommend)[26] you ask your employer for a few days' holiday. And you should cut out the alcohol.

ALAN: But I (try)[27] to. I used to drink even more.

DOCTOR: Right, well, I'm going to prescribe you some pills to help you sleep. They (contain)[28] a sedative and an anti-depressant. You (need)[29] to take them three times a day, after meals. Do that and then come and see me again in a couple of weeks and we'll see how you (get on)[30].

ALAN: OK, thank you very much.

# 17 *Relative clauses*

## Defining relative clauses

*1* Defining relative clauses identify which person, people or things we are talking about.

We use *who* or *that* to identify people.
*The person **who/that** invented the wheel was a genius.*

To refer to things we use *which* or *that*.
*A hotline is a service **that/which** enables computer users to get help.*

To refer to places and time we use *where* and *when*.
*The Tate Modern is a gallery **where** you can see a lot of famous modern art.*
*Thanksgiving is the time **when** Americans get together with family and friends.*

*Whose* indicates possession.
*Anyone **whose** credit card is lost or stolen should report it immediately.*

*2* If the relative pronoun is the <u>object</u> of a defining relative clause, it can be left out.
*She's the person <u>who/that</u> I met in Rio.*
→ *She's the person I met in Rio.*
*The newspaper <u>which</u> I read is called The China Daily.*
→ *The newspaper I read is called The China Daily.*

## Non-defining relative clauses

Non-defining relative clauses add information. We use *who* to introduce extra information about people and *which* for things. *That* is not possible in sentences of this type. The relative clause is separated from the main clause by commas.
*Marc Andreessen, **who** co-founded Netscape, is one of the most intelligent men in the United States.*
*Our firm, **which** made record profits last year, is rapidly downsizing.*

## Reduced relative clauses

Relative clauses can be shortened by using a present participle when the verb is active.
*Microsoft is a company **that makes** huge profits.*
→ *Microsoft is a company **making** huge profits.*

A past participle is used when the verb is passive.
*We've launched a new perfume, **which is called** Island Moon.*
→ *We've launched a new perfume, **called** Island Moon.*

## PRACTICE

**1** Complete the questions with a relative pronoun and then answer them, as in the example.

### Quiz

What do we call a person *that/who* has a billion dollars?
Answer: *a billionaire*

**a** What do we call someone _____ buys and sells shares for someone else?
Answer: _____

**b** What is the name of the company _____ was co-founded by Jim Clark?
Answer: _____

**c** What is the name of the place outside San Francisco _____ the computer industry is located?
Answer: _____

**d** What is the name of the man _____ company, Computer Associates, made $670 million in 1999?
Answer: _____

**e** What do we call a sum of money _____ is paid to an executive when he or she leaves a company?
Answer: _____

**f** What do we call top executives _____ pay is often considered excessive?
Answer: _____

**g** What do we call a person _____ uses the Internet to buy and sell shares in a single day?
Answer: _____

**2** Shorten these sentences by using a present or past participle to make a reduced relative clause.

*1* Relay plc is a start-up company which sells software for mobile phones.

*2* The cable that links the two machines caught fire.

*3* The building which was damaged during the storm will have to be pulled down.

*4* All the people who were previously employed in manual jobs have been retrained.

*5* The summit meeting that takes place in Ottawa next week will make some important decisions.

*6* The men who are being sent on this mission will receive danger money.

## 18  Reported speech

*1* We use reported speech to say what someone else said at a different time or place. The verb form depends on the time of the report.
*Brian: 'I **want** to join the team.'*
*Brian **says** he **wants** to join the team.*

(The situation and the reporting verb are in the present, so the verb in the reported speech clause is in the present.)

*2* When using a reporting verb in the past, we generally backshift the tense of the verb in the reported speech clause. In other words, we move it back one step in the past, from present to past or present perfect to past perfect. However, there are no absolute rules about this, and we may leave a verb in the present to emphasise that a situation hasn't changed.
*Brian **said** he **wanted/wants** to join the team.*
*'I**'ve** talked to the boss.'*
*He said he **had** talked to the boss.*

*'I'm sorry I **didn't warn** you earlier.'*
*He told me he **was** sorry he **didn't warn/hadn't warned** me earlier.*

(If the original verb is already in the past tense, it is not necessary to use the past perfect.)

*3* When we want to convey the speaker's attitude or intention, we use reporting verbs other than *say* or *tell*. These verbs may be followed by a structure other than a *that* clause.
*'Of course we'll pay compensation.'*
*They **assured** the firm that they would pay compensation.*

*'I've absolutely no idea where the money's gone.'*
*She **claimed** not to know where the money had gone.*
    *(She **claimed** that she didn't know...)*

*'I really do think that I should have a rise.'*
*She **insisted** on being given a rise. (She **insisted** that she was given...)*

*'I think you can see there have been mistakes in the method of calculation.'*
*He **pointed out** that there had been mistakes in the method of calculation.*

*'Why don't we take on some temporary staff?'*
*She **suggested** taking on some temporary staff.*
    *(She **suggested** that we took on...)*

*'We'll take you to court if you don't pay up.'*
*They **threatened** to take us to court if we didn't pay up.*

**1** Complete the dialogues using the information in direct speech, as in the example.
'It's not going to rain in the afternoon.'
A: You haven't brought an umbrella!
B: *But you said that it wasn't going to rain this afternoon.*

*1* 'I've just got back from New York.'
   A: Actually I've never been to the United States.
   B: But earlier on you said _____

*2* 'Sandra left the company three weeks ago.'
   A: I'll give your report to Sandra when I see her.
   B: But you just said _____

*3* 'No thanks, I'm not thirsty.'
   A: Where's <u>my</u> coffee?
   B: But you told me _____

*4* 'Michael says that he doesn't know how the money was spent.'
   A: Michael will tell you how the money was spent.
   B: But you said he claims _____

*5* 'If there are any problems, we'll refund your money in full.'
   A: I'm sorry, but we can't give you your money back on this product.
   B: But you assured me _____

**2** Match the two sentence halves.
*1* He warned
*2* She suggested
*3* The firm offered
*4* They threatened
*5* We insisted
*6* She pointed out

*a* to sue us.
*b* taking on some extra staff.
*c* that the boss was angry about something.
*d* me not to sell my shares yet.
*e* on a new date for the launch.
*f* to double his take-home pay.

# 1 first impressions

*GRAMMAR REVIEW* **page 7**
*Who are they?*

Michael Milken was the hero of the world's financial markets in the 1980s. He invented the market for 'junk bonds' – high yield, high risk bonds – and made a fortune as a result. In one year he earned an incredible $550 million. Milken's junk bonds allowed businesspeople to borrow enormous amounts of money which they often used to launch takeovers of some of America's biggest corporations. But Milken's enemies believed that Milken wasn't making his money entirely honestly. His dealings were so complicated that it was hard to find out exactly how he was operating. But after a long investigation, a New York court found him guilty of using secret information in his financial dealings, and in November 1990, a judge sent him to prison for ten years.

Milken's time in prison changed many things about him – including his appearance. Before he went to prison, he used to wear a false hairpiece. When he came out, he stopped wearing it and showed the world that he was completely bald!

Darius Guppy used to be a part of British high society. He came from a wealthy family and studied at Oxford University where he became the best friend of Princess Diana's brother, Earl Spencer. But when London's Lloyd's insurance market ran into problems in the early 1990s, Guppy's family were financially ruined and Guppy decided to follow a career in business.

He raised some money from investors and started a small company that bought and sold gems and precious stones. But Guppy was soon in trouble again. While he was working in New York, a man threatened him with a gun and robbed him of precious stones worth nearly £2 million. Fortunately, Guppy was insured and claimed the money from his insurance company.

At the age of twenty-five, Guppy was again a wealthy man. But the robbery was not all it seemed. A police investigation showed that it was a trick to get the insurance money and Guppy was soon under arrest. In March 1993 the man who used to go to parties with the British royal family woke up in prison, facing a sentence of five years for fraud.

Nicola Horlick is known in the British media as a superwoman. In her mid-thirties, she was one of the top fund managers in the City of London, responsible for around £18 billion of other people's money. She earned over a million pounds a year as well as having a successful marriage and five children.

She hit the headlines at the end of 1996, when her bank, Deutsche Morgan Grenfell, suspended her from her well-paid job. They said she was planning to leave the company and to take several of its star employees with her. Horlick was furious. She believed that the bank was acting unfairly. So she hired a public relations consultant to tell her side of the story to the newspapers and then flew to Frankfurt to talk to the bank's bosses face to face.

Although she left Deutsche Morgan Grenfell soon after the incident, her public argument with them had made her famous and she soon found a job as a fund manager with another bank and resumed her position as the superwoman of British business life.

*DOING BUSINESS 2* **page 13**
*Two ruses*

**CALL 1**

| | |
|---|---|
| RECEP 1 | Hey, this is Thorosoft. Julie speaking. How may I help you? |
| RUSER | Oh hi, Julie. My name's Rachel Bethania. Now, I know this probably sounds a little strange, but last night I was playing tennis and got into a doubles game with one of your programmers. |
| RECEP 1 | Uh-huh. |
| RUSER | The thing is, I gave him a ride home in my car but he left his tennis racquet behind. |
| RECEP 1 | Uh-huh. |
| RUSER | Now I can't remember his name. Dave or Don or something. |
| RECEP 1 | Can't help you I'm afraid, honey. |
| RUSER | I'm sorry? I just want to give him back his tennis racquet. |
| RECEP 1 | You're rusing me, ain't you? |
| RUSER | I'm sorry. What do you mean? Of course I'm not. |
| RECEP 1 | Oh, honey, you are. Thorosoft's an all-female concern. |

Sure as hell ain't nobody goes by the name of Dave or Don in this company.

RUSER Ah ... Well, yes, it was pretty dark by that time, so ...

## CALL 2

RECEP 2 Good morning. You're through to Glocom-Prog.

RUSER Hello? Hello?

RECEP 2 Hello. You're through to Glocom-Prog.

RUSER Ah, great. I'm just checking a few of your lines here.

RECEP 2 I'm sorry, who am I speaking to?

RUSER I'm the one in the yellow hat at the top of the pole outside your window.

RECEP 2 I'm sorry, I'm in the Glocom-Prog reception. We don't have any windows.

RUSER Hey, well, you're probably the lucky one. It's pouring with rain out here and I want to get back down to earth and inside just as soon as I can.

RECEP 2 You're seriously up a telephone pole outside the building ... in this weather?

RUSER Yeah. And I'm not up here for my health, you understand?

RECEP 2 I'm sorry, yeah.

RUSER Now, we've had reports of a few problems with some of the extensions for the people in your programming area.

RECEP 2 Programming area?

RUSER Well, whatever you call it. Could you just read out the names and extension numbers of your main programmers?

RECEP 2 Well, I can't really do that.

RUSER Look, I'm not going to hang on up here arguing with you. Either you give me their numbers, or they don't get their lines working. Now, what's it to be?

RECEP 2 Well, yeah ... I guess ... Just give me a second, I'll get the names and numbers you want up on the screen ...

# 2 managing change

## GRAMMAR REVIEW   page 19
### Complaining about change

MAN 1 Well, I don't think it's right. She can't just march in here and start telling us to rearrange things like that.

MAN 2 Quite. She's only been with this company two minutes.

MAN 1 She hasn't listened to our ideas, has she?

MAN 2 She hasn't seen the way we work.

MAN 1 In fact, she hasn't taken the time to get to know us at all.

MAN 2 The trouble is that ever since she joined she's just been rushing around like a lunatic.

MAN 1 Yes, she's been having all those meetings with senior management, hasn't she? Certainly not with us.

MAN 2 And she's been travelling constantly. Amsterdam one day, Frankfurt the next. Very nice for some, but we've hardly seen her.

MAN 1 Anyway, she's gone too far this time.

MAN 2 Absolutely.

MAN 1 And that plant ... that plant has always been in the corner of this office.

MAN 2 It's certainly been here as long as I've been working here, which is a number of years, I can tell you.

MAN 1 Anyway, as far as I'm concerned, if that plant goes, I go too!

MAN 2 Quite right ... Quite right, too ... Another cup of tea?

# 3 the boss

## DOING BUSINESS 1   page 35
### Delegating styles

WOMAN Mark, have you got a moment?

MAN Yeah, sure.

WOMAN Listen, I know this is late in the day, but I wonder if you'd be able to fly out and make the presentation this weekend.

MAN But I thought you were going to do that.

WOMAN Well, yes, I was, but I'm incredibly busy at the moment. You know how it is.

MAN This weekend? Couldn't John go? He knows all there is to know about the project.

WOMAN Yeah, but he doesn't know the people and he doesn't know the city. The thing is, Mark, I think you're the right person for the job. I hope you're OK about that.

MAN I get the message. I'm on the payroll. Do I have a choice?

WOMAN Thanks, Mark.

MAN Yeah.

## ISSUES   page 38
### An expensive education

Thomas Watson Senior was the man who built the giant computer company, IBM. Under his leadership, the company became famous for its strong values and tradition of customer service. The people who worked there were expected to be dedicated corporate men and women who could always be recognised by their dark blue suits.

On one occasion, a young IBM executive had involved the company in an extremely risky business venture. Unfortunately, the project had gone badly wrong and the company lost $10 million. Thomas Watson, of course, wanted an explanation and he called the young executive into his office. The young man stood nervously in front of his boss's desk.

'I suppose you want my resignation,' he said miserably.

'You must be joking,' Watson replied. 'We've just spent $10 million on your education.'

# 4 face to face

## DOING BUSINESS 2    page 48
### The Iron Lady

GARDNER   Will we ever return to full employment, Prime Minister ... what is known as full employment?

THATCHER   I don't know. It depends on your definition of 'full employment'. I believe that when we're through this period, the same enterprise that created jobs in the past with new technology will once again come and create new jobs of the future. You see if you look at it, the first industrial revolution, people were frightened, machinery, they thought, took their jobs. But machinery gave us a whole new standard of living. And then we got the computer age just after the war. I remember Leon Bagret coming out with the age of automation. And people were frightened that computers would take jobs but they created jobs. Now we've got the microchip age and they're frightened. But I believe that just as in the past, new jobs will be created through new products, so in the future.

## DOING BUSINESS 2    page 48
### A straight answer

**1**

INTERVIEWER   Will we ever return to full employment?

INTERVIEWEE   Yes, I think we will return to full employment some time in the next ten years. That's because a large number of hi-tech industries are setting up in our country at the moment. For example, last week an American company opened a silicon chip plant that will provide jobs for over three and a half thousand people.

**2**   [repeat of Thatcher's answer from *The Iron Lady*]

## DOING BUSINESS 2    page 49
### Q = A + 1

**QUESTION AND ANSWER 1**

SHAREHOLDER   Can you explain why the company is planning to shut down another factory at the end of next month?

CEO   Very simply, the plant that you're referring to has been running at a loss for the past two years. But the key point here is that our rationalisation strategy has produced record profits for the company over the past two quarters. And it's a strategy that we certainly intend to pursue.

**QUESTION AND ANSWER 2**

MANAGER   Is it true that everyone in your department was out at lunch for over three hours last Friday?

SALESWOMAN   Well yes I must admit that we did all have a long lunch. But the important thing is, we had something to celebrate! For the third month running, everybody achieved their sales target!

MANAGER   Oh, I see. Well I suppose that is worth celebrating, isn't it?

**QUESTION AND ANSWER 3**

JOURNALIST   Why has the government again decided to increase taxes on fuel, when businesses have been asking for a reduction in these rates for years?

POLITICIAN   Well, first let me say that the adjustments we made to the fuel tax are very much in line with inflation. But the facts of the matter are that business is better off under this government than it has been at any time for the past twenty years. Corporation tax is down, we've slashed bureaucracy, interest rates are at their lowest for a decade ...

## DOING BUSINESS 2    page 49
### Thatcher again

DIMBLEBY   You don't think that the slogan now sounds rather tattered – 'popular capitalism'?

THATCHER   Not at all ... not at all. The stock market is back down to where it was something like fifteen months ago. No. That slogan is not tattered. We shall go on expanding and extending capitalism ... popular capitalism and it will give many many people an extra income when they retire and something to hand on to their children. Look at the results that are coming now ... ah, you want me to stop.

DIMBLEBY   I ...

THATCHER   The results are good, I'll not go into any detail.

DIMBLEBY   It is always interesting to hear you going on, Prime Minister, but I want to move on actually to the next subject if we can, to the Health Service ...

THATCHER   But you don't want me to go on and on. I understand.

DIMBLEBY   That's extremely good of you.

# 5 risk and reward

## GRAMMAR REVIEW    page 54
### Mosaic

In early 1994, when Marc Andreessen was just twenty-three years old, he arrived in California's Silicon Valley with an idea that would change the world. As a student at the University of Illinois, he and his friends had developed a program called Mosaic, which allowed people to share information on the World Wide Web.

Before Mosaic, the Web had been used mainly by scientists and other technical people who were happy just to send and receive text. But with Mosaic, Andreessen and his friends had developed a program which could send images over the Web as well.

Mosaic was an overnight success. It was put on the university's network at the beginning of 1993 and by the end of the year it had over a million users.

But Andreessen was frustrated. Although he and his friends had done all the work to develop Mosaic, it was his bosses at the university who were getting all the credit.

So, in early 1994, Andreessen left the University of Illinois, where he had spent many happy years, and went to seek his fortune in Silicon Valley.

## *GRAMMAR REVIEW*   **page 54**
### *Andreessen and Clark*

Soon after Andreessen arrived in Silicon Valley, he started to have meetings with a man called Jim Clark, who was one of the Valley's most famous entrepreneurs. Clark had founded a company called Silicon Graphics, which produced big computer systems that were used by Hollywood film studios and aircraft and car designers. In early 1994, nobody was making any real money from the Internet, which was still very slow and hard to use. But Andreessen had seen an opportunity that would make him and Clark rich men within two years. He suggested they should create a new computer program that would do the same job as Mosaic but would be much easier to use. He pointed out that the Internet would soon have over fifty million users, who would all be potential customers for their idea. Clark listened carefully to Andreessen, whose ideas and enthusiasm impressed him greatly.

Eventually, Clark agreed to invest $3 million of his own money in the project and to raise an extra 15 million from venture capitalists, who were always keen to listen to Clark's new ideas.

## *GRAMMAR REVIEW*   **page 55**
### *The birth of Netscape*

Clark and Andreessen decided to call their new company Netscape, and soon their offices were full of young software engineers working day and night to complete the new program. In October 1994, Netscape launched its new browser, called Navigator, and by the following summer it had over ten million users. The success of the Netscape Navigator persuaded Clark that they should offer shares for sale to the general public, allowing the company to raise a great deal of extra money.

When Netscape's shares went on sale in August 1995, their value increased by three times in just one day, making it the most successful share offer in history. The Netscape shares owned by the company's two founders had made them rich beyond their wildest dreams: Jim Clark had become a billionaire and Marc Andreessen, at the age of just twenty-four, was worth over $80 million.

## *DOING BUSINESS 1*   **page 59**
### *Business voices*

**1**

HAWKINGS  I guess if I look at a share price and the statistics associated with it, I would consider probably the most important as the P/E ratio, which gives an indication of how profitable the company is. However, if I was looking for a share as an investment to give me an income, the yield would be very significant. I might also consider the highs and the lows as an indication of volatility and the volume as an indication of activity.

**2**

BROOKS  I'd look at two of the factors on here. I'd look at the price/earnings multiple but also I'd look at the change in the price between the high and the low points during the year. The price/earnings multiple is interesting if you know what the comparison is with other companies in the same sector, but I also like to think that I'm buying into value of a company so I like to buy at a low point in its price during the last year. I don't want to buy at the highest price.

# 6 persuasion

## *VOCABULARY*   **page 69**
### *On the doorstep*

**CONVERSATION 1**

WOMAN  Hello.

SALESMAN  Good evening. Mrs Knight?

WOMAN  Yes?

SALESMAN  Yes. I'm with the Wide Windows Company. It's about an enquiry you made ... concerning new windows.

WOMAN  New windows? No, I'm sorry that doesn't ring a bell with me.

SALESMAN  Then maybe your husband got in touch with us?

WOMAN  No, I don't think so. He hasn't told me anything about it, anyway.

SALESMAN  Ah. Well ... Well, I don't want to keep you but perhaps I could just take you through the special offer that we're running this month.

WOMAN  Oh, I'm sorry, I haven't got time to listen to a long sales pitch this evening.

SALESMAN  No, please, hold on just a moment. I can give you a feel for what we're offering in just ... just a couple of minutes.

WOMAN  No, really. You're speaking to the wrong person.

SALESMAN  Please, it ...

WOMAN  No, I'm sorry. I hear what you're saying, but we're just not interested. Well, thank you for calling, but no.

SALESMAN  Well, thank you, Mrs Knight. Goodbye.

WOMAN  Goodbye.

## CONVERSATION 2

MAN  Hello?

SALESWOMAN  Good evening. Mr Morrison?

MAN  Yes.

SALESWOMAN  I'm from the Wide Windows Company. I wanted to see if you were still interested in some new windows.

MAN  New windows? Oh yes, I dimly remember my wife showing me something about that.

SALESWOMAN  Perhaps it was our brochure. Is this what you saw?

MAN  Ah, yes. Yes, that's it.

SALESWOMAN  And did you have a chance to look at it?

MAN  Well, I did, but ... Well, let me be perfectly clear about this. My wife and I don't really see eye to eye on this one. From my point of view the windows we've got now are absolutely fine. But she would probably paint a completely different picture.

SALESWOMAN  I see.

MAN  But I'm afraid that she's out this evening.

SALESWOMAN  Ah. Well, perhaps I'll leave this brochure with you anyway. You can have a look through it and if you like what you see, I'll be happy to come back some other time.

MAN  Of course. Thank you. Goodbye.

SALESWOMAN  Goodbye.

## *DOING BUSINESS 1*  page 70
### *Buying a car*

SALESWOMAN  Morning, sir. Can I help you?

CUSTOMER  Yuh. I'm interested in a coupe.

SALESWOMAN  A coupe. Absolutely.

CUSTOMER  Only I don't see one.

SALESWOMAN  No, that's because it's just up the road at the moment, at our showroom in Mahopac. Would you like us to bring it down for you right now?

CUSTOMER  Mahopac?

SALESWOMAN  Oh it's no distance. It's only ... well, less than an hour away, in fact.

CUSTOMER  Well, I don't have a lot of time.

SALESWOMAN  I tell you what. Why don't you sit down and have a cup of coffee? Then I'll take you through the

brochure, here. By the time I've told you a little bit more about the car, it'll be waiting outside.

CUSTOMER  Well ... yeah, OK. Why not?

## *DOING BUSINESS 1*  page 70
### *Overcoming objections*

### SITUATION 1

SALESWOMAN  So, that's the system we're proposing. What do you think?

DIRECTOR  Well, thank you for that. I was certainly very interested by what you said, and I'm sure the other directors were, too. But, this is a big decision for us and we really need some time to think about it.

SALESWOMAN  Of course, I quite understand. And I realise it must be difficult for you to come to a decision while I'm here. Why don't I go out for a cup of coffee and give you a chance to talk about it and then I can come back in ... what shall I say ... twenty minutes?

DIRECTOR  Well, I was really thinking ... well, yes, why not? If everyone agrees? Is that OK?

### SITUATION 2

WOMAN  Oh, I'm sorry, you know, I really can't make up my mind. They're lovely, but a dog's a lot of work. And it's such a big commitment.

MAN  I tell you what, you don't have to make a firm decision now. Why don't you just take one home with you for a couple of days?

WOMAN  Could I?

MAN  Yes, of course. You can see how you get along together, and if things work out, you can keep her. If it doesn't work out, bring her back, no problem.

WOMAN  Oh that's a really good idea. Thank you, that's really kind of you. Well, I think we'll take this one here. Hello ...

### SITUATION 3

MAN  No, thank you very much. It's a very nice television, but I'm afraid it's just too expensive for us, isn't it, dear?

WOMAN  Oh, yes, too expensive, I'm afraid. There are much cheaper ones, you know.

SALESMAN  OK. If this TV was the same price as our competitor's TVs, would you buy it then?

MAN  Well, well, yes, I suppose I might.

SALESMAN  Why is that?

MAN  Well, because obviously, as you say, it's a very good television.

SALESMAN  But don't you think it's worth paying a little bit extra to get the kind of TV that you want? After all, you don't buy one every day.

MAN  No, very true.

| | |
|---|---|
| WOMAN | Perhaps if it was just a bit cheaper, we might think about it. |
| SALESMAN | Hmm. I don't know. There could be some flexibility here, though. Let me see what I can do for you. |

## DOING BUSINESS 2    page 72
### Assessing a salesman

| | |
|---|---|
| SALESMAN | Well, you sign the service agreement and, er, and you pay and, well, that's it. |
| CUSTOMER | Good. |
| SALESMAN | Oh, how are you paying by the way? |
| CUSTOMER | Credit card? |
| SALESMAN | Of course. You won't regret this, Mr Earnshaw, these really are the best little portable machines on the market. |
| CUSTOMER | Yes, as you said … |
| SALESMAN | I've got one myself actually. Never had a moment's trouble with it. |
| CUSTOMER | Excellent. |
| SALESMAN | Oh yes. You made the right choice, Mr Earnshaw. Lovely machines. The screen is one of the best I've ever seen actually. Sharp as a pin. Beautiful. Good choice. Now, where are we? Yes. Here's the service agreement. Right. I'll just take you through this. So, in the first paragraph here, you'll notice that we're offering you a full 24-hour helpline should you have any problems with the machines. I mean, you won't, but if you need us, we can guarantee you that we'll always be there for you. Now you don't need to worry too much about the second paragraph – that really refers more to our higher-end models … |
| CUSTOMER | Actually, I'm sorry, but I'm a little pushed for time. |
| SALESMAN | This won't take a moment. |
| CUSTOMER | Look, I'm sorry, but I am in rather a hurry. Um … I tell you what, do you mind if I pop out now and then perhaps I could come back later and we can sort out the payment and the other details then? |
| SALESMAN | Of course, Mr Earnshaw. No problem. We're open until eight tonight. I'll put the machines on one side for you. |
| CUSTOMER | Thank you. |
| SALESMAN | It's a pleasure, Mr Earnshaw. I'll see you later. Have a good day. |
| CUSTOMER | Yes. Thank you. Goodbye. |

## ISSUES    page 74
### Ordinary Powder

In the late 1990s, the big American company Proctor & Gamble was spending large amounts of money advertising its Ariel washing powder in Russia. Its TV commercials were very successful and demonstrated the effectiveness of Ariel by comparing it to an 'ordinary powder'.

Then one day a person working for a Russian manufacturer of washing powder in Angarsk, Siberia, had a bright idea. Why not call the washing powder made by his company 'Ordinary Powder'? That way, they could benefit from millions of dollars of advertising provided by their huge American competitor, without spending a rouble themselves. Of course, P & G's adverts showed that 'ordinary powder' wasn't as good as Ariel, but the company figured that didn't matter too much – they could sell their powder at a fraction of the price of the American powder.

And the marketing men from Angarsk were absolutely right. The Russians admired the cheek of the Siberian company – and within a few months their 'Ordinary Powder' had come from nowhere to capture a significant slice of the market.

# 7    paranoia

## GRAMMAR REVIEW    page 78
### A manager's nightmare

Unnh … Three o'clock … Mmm … Three o'clock tomorrow … Mmm … At three o'clock tomorrow, I'll be sitting in that meeting. And they … they won't have taken a decision, will they? They'll all be saying, 'Well, we liked your proposal, but we need some time to think about it.' We need some time to think about it! … Time to think … They'll have had my proposal for a month by then. No, they'll have had it for over a month. Over a month, for Heaven's sake. Heaven's sake … For Heaven's … Unnh … Mmm … Three o'clock … Mmm … Over a month … Unnh … And they won't be thinking about the competition, will they? They won't be thinking about the competition! I know that other lot will have had the same idea … Unnh … I know it. And that other lot won't be having planning meetings. Oh no. They'll be doing something about it. They'll have already agreed the budget. They'll be building prototypes. They'll have started work on the marketing plan. And they'll be leaving us further and further behind … Further and further behind … Further and further … Unnh … I can see it. I can see it now. This time next year, they'll have had the launch party. They'll be running their first advertising campaign. They'll have had articles in the press. Oh yes, they'll be sitting pretty. They'll be sitting pretty … And what will I be doing? I'll be looking for a new job, won't I? … I'll be looking for a new job … A new job … A new job … A new job … Mmm. Oooh.

# 8 the **deal**

## DOING BUSINESS 2   page 96
### Five negotiations

### NEGOTIATION 1

**PERSON 1**   Well, I must say that I think six per cent is a perfectly fair discount.

**PERSON 2**   Frankly, I don't think there's any point in us continuing with this discussion. There are lots of other people out there offering exactly the same services as you and at much better prices.

**PERSON 1**   I'm sorry, but ...

**PERSON 2**   Just listen to me for a minute, will you? Either you give me ten per cent, or I take my business elsewhere. Am I making myself clear?

**PERSON 1**   Perfectly ...

**PERSON 2**   Am I making myself clear?

### NEGOTIATION 2

**PERSON 3**   Right then, I think that just about wraps it up. Do we have a deal?

**PERSON 4**   Absolutely. It's been a pleasure doing business with you.

**PERSON 3**   And you.

**PERSON 4**   Oh, just one last thing – it won't be a problem if we increase my discount by half a per cent, will it?

**PERSON 3**   Um ...

**PERSON 4**   Only I've been thinking, it's going to make my life so much easier ...

### NEGOTIATION 3

**PERSON 5**   Well, it looks great. It's just the kind of service we want.

**PERSON 6**   Fantastic.

**PERSON 5**   But for me, the problem is the level of discount. As I said, I need seven per cent.

**PERSON 6**   Hmm. That is a problem. I'm afraid I can't take any kind of decision about discounts. I'm going to have to speak to my boss about this. But, well ... she's not going to like it.

### NEGOTIATION 4

**PERSON 7**   So, that's the deal. Believe me, you won't find a better offer anywhere else.

**PERSON 8**   Well, perhaps I'll think about it.

**PERSON 7**   Look, I don't want you to feel that you're under any pressure, but this offer's not going to be here forever.

**PERSON 8**   What do you mean?

**PERSON 7**   Well, this is the very last machine that we've got in stock. If you don't order today, I simply can't guarantee that it'll be here tomorrow.

**PERSON 8**   I see.

**PERSON 7**   And all the prices are going up next week anyway.

**PERSON 8**   Hmm.

**PERSON 7**   So, what do you say?

### NEGOTIATION 5

**PERSON 9**   Well, in principle, I like the sound of the idea, but the devil's always in the detail, isn't it? Now, what I'd like to do is talk through some of the small print.

**PERSON 10**   OK, here's the situation. I've got a flight back to New York at half past four, which means that I'm going to have to leave in half an hour ... forty minutes at the very latest.

**PERSON 9**   So, what are you saying?

**PERSON 10**   I've got to tie up this deal before I leave. You know what's on offer – it's your decision.

## ISSUES   page 98
### Arlen's lucky day

In the 1940s, a man called Michael Arlen was trying to write scripts for Hollywood movies. He'd had some success, but he was finding it very hard to make a living. Then one day, he went for a drink at a fashionable New York restaurant. In the lobby he saw the famous Hollywood film mogul, Sam Goldwyn. Arlen knew that Goldwyn owned one of Hollywood's biggest studios, so he went up to him and explained his problems.

'In your situation,' Sam Goldwyn told him, 'you should buy racehorses.'

Arlen hardly had enough money for a drink, so Goldwyn's advice was no help at all. Then, to his amazement, on the other side of the restaurant, he saw Sam Goldwyn's great rival, Louis B. Mayer, who owned another top Hollywood studio at that time. Again Arlen introduced himself.

'So what are your plans for the future?' asked Mayer.

'Well,' said Arlen, 'I was just talking to Sam Goldwyn ...'

Mayer immediately interrupted him: 'How much did he offer you?'

Thinking quickly, Arlen said, 'Not enough.'

'Would you take fifteen thousand dollars for thirty weeks?' asked Mayer.

In those days, that was a very large salary and Arlen didn't hesitate: 'Yes,' he said.

# 9 **globalisation**

## GRAMMAR REVIEW   page 102
### Black Wednesday

**PRESENTER**   On Wednesday 16 September 1992, Britain's finance minister, Chancellor of the Exchequer

LAMONT    Norman Lamont, walked out of a meeting with the Prime Minister, John Major, and told journalists of an astonishing change in government policy. Britain, he said, had taken the decision to withdraw from the European Exchange Rate Mechanism – or ERM. Today has been an extremely difficult and turbulent day. Massive speculative flows have continued to disrupt the functioning of the Exchange Rate Mechanism. The government has concluded that Britain's best interests are served by suspending our membership of the Exchange Rate Mechanism.

PRESENTER    Some say that John Major's government never recovered from the events of that day. Membership of the ERM had been a key part of government policy and from that moment the public's confidence in his government began to disappear. Many believe that if Black Wednesday had never happened, Tony Blair would never have become prime minister.

*GRAMMAR REVIEW*    **page 103**
*The man who broke the pound*

PRESENTER    Immediately after Black Wednesday, the person with the biggest smile on his face was a Hungarian-American called George Soros. Soros had been one of the most successful and respected operators in the financial markets for many years, but if it hadn't been for Black Wednesday, he might not have come to the attention of the world's media.

The fact of the matter is that in 1992 Soros did more than anyone else to break the pound. That summer, he became more and more convinced that the value of the pound was much too high. He believed that it would be forced to leave the ERM and that its value would fall. And he was prepared to bet that he was right. So at the beginning of September, he borrowed £5 billion and changed it into German marks at a rate of 2.79 Deutschmarks to the pound. He then simply waited. It was obviously a big risk, but Soros wasn't worried. In an interview, he explained what would have happened if he had been wrong.

SOROS    Well, we would have lost ... we would have lost some money. Nothing like the money we made. And of course this was a bet ... what is called a one-way bet. Because the loss would have been very small and the profit was ... was very large.

PRESENTER    Of course, events proved that Soros was absolutely right. Soon after Black Wednesday Soros simply changed his German marks back into British pounds – this time at a rate of 2.5 Deutschmarks to the pound. The result was a profit to Soros and a loss to the British people of a cool $1 billion.

In an interview soon afterwards, Soros defended his actions.

SOROS    And I have absolutely no sense of guilt, I can assure you, because had I not taken the position, somebody else would have taken the position. And so it ... it ... it just happens that I played the game better or bigger than other people. But the unfortunate fact is that there is a loss to the British government out of this.

PRESENTER    A billion dollars richer and a clear conscience. All in a day's work for the man who broke the pound.

*DOING BUSINESS 2*    **page 109**
*Telling a joke*

### THE OLDEST JOB

One day a farmer, an architect and a lawyer were having a discussion about what was the oldest job in the world.

The farmer said, 'The job of a farmer is clearly the oldest in the world. After all, food is our most basic need – before we started farming, we had to live off roots and berries. Before farmers, we would all have been constantly hungry.'

The architect shook his head. 'I don't agree,' he said. 'The job of an architect is far older. When you think about it, our most basic need is to have shelter, to have a roof over our head – the truth is that architects were the first people to protect us from all the chaos and confusion of the world.'

At this, the lawyer smiled and said, 'And who do you think created the chaos and confusion in the first place?'

# 10 vision

*DOING BUSINESS 1*    **page 118**
*Starting a presentation*

### EXTRACT 1

TOM PETERS    Good evening. It's a pleasure to be here with you. Ian, in his remarks, referred kindly to me as one of the quote 'numerous breed of American students of the science of management'. I am afraid that I would view that frankly as a most dubious distinction. It is a little discussed fact that America's market share has increased in management consulting, business school graduates and management publications exactly at the time that our market share in the real world of hard goods and services has decreased.

## *DOING BUSINESS 1*   page 119
### *Innovation*

**EXTRACT 2**

TOM PETERS   Now, the other part of the innovation story which makes it tough, is not only is, it's a numbers game, but we totally depend on irrational people. I mean, the reality is that the odds of a successful innovation making it to market are zero. Therefore, if you were a so-called expected-value thinker, you would never start. We depend on people who see the world irrationally.

I mean, George Bernard Shaw may in fact have said it best. The marvellous comment that he made a while back, is he said, and this was in *Man and Superman:* 'The reasonable man adapts himself to the world. The unreasonable man persists in trying to adapt the world to himself. Therefore, all progress depends on the unreasonable man.'

No problem, except we go out of our way to fire unreasonable men within all of our organisations.

Philip Villers, the founder of Computer Vision and other firms, defined entrepreneurship in much the same terms. His definition of entrepreneurship: 'Unreasonable commitment based upon inadequate evidence.'

And that again is deadly serious. That's what we're dealing with, that's what we're talking about and it is the antithesis of the way we typically run our businesses.

### *Emphasis*

**EXTRACT 2.1**

TOM PETERS   ... we totally depend on irrational people. I mean, the reality is that the odds of a successful innovation making it to market are zero. Therefore, if you were a so-called expected-value thinker, you would never start. We depend on people who see the world irrationally.

### *Pausing*

**EXTRACT 2.2**

TOM PETERS   And that again is deadly serious. That's what we're dealing with, that's what we're talking about and it is the antithesis of the way we typically run our businesses.

### *Pausing and emphasis*

**EXTRACT 2.3**

TOM PETERS   'The reasonable man adapts himself to the world. The unreasonable man persists in trying to adapt the world to himself. Therefore all progress depends on the unreasonable man.'

No problem, except we go out of our way to fire unreasonable men within all of our organisations.

## *DOING BUSINESS 2*   page 120
### *Introducing the theme*

**EXTRACT 3**

TOM PETERS   You hear it here first tonight. I am that rare person in the world who is able to predict with certainty the price of oil next year at this time. I will personally guarantee you that it will either be seven or forty-seven dollars a barrel. I will likewise guarantee you that if it's forty-seven, it'll be seven the year afterwards and if it's seven, it'll be forty-seven the year afterwards.

The point being that throughout the economies of the industrialised world we are beset with a degree of ambiguity, uncertainty and madness never before seen.

And why that is so significant is that our organisations are designed in a perverse way to not be able to deal with that.

The organisational model is the standard average chugalong Henry Ford production-line model and in fact we're now required to build organisations that welcome, love and cherish ambiguity and reorganisation on a weekly basis, rather than a once a decade basis.

It is a crazy time indeed.

### *Humour and surprise*

**EXTRACT 3.1**

TOM PETERS   You hear it here first tonight. I am that rare person in the world who is able to predict with certainty the price of oil next year at this time. I will personally guarantee you that it will either be seven or forty-seven dollars a barrel. I will likewise guarantee you that if it's forty-seven, it'll be seven the year afterwards and if it's seven, it'll be forty-seven the year afterwards.

### *Groups of three*

[repeat of the whole of Extract 3]

# grammar key

## 1 Articles

**1**

| | | | |
|---|---|---|---|
| 1 | an | 5 | The, the |
| 2 | a | 6 | Ø |
| 3 | the, Ø, a | 7 | A, a |
| 4 | Ø | 8 | A, a, Ø |

**2**

| | | | | | | | |
|---|---|---|---|---|---|---|---|
| 1 | A | 6 | a | 11 | Ø | 16 | the |
| 2 | a | 7 | the | 12 | the | 17 | the |
| 3 | Ø | 8 | an | 13 | the | 18 | the |
| 4 | Ø | 9 | the | 14 | a | 19 | the |
| 5 | Ø | 10 | A | 15 | The | 20 | Ø |

## 2 Conditionals (1)

**1**  1 d   2 a   3 b   4 c

**2**  1 a   2 e   3 d   4 b   5 c

**3**
2  If I won the lottery, I'd buy a yacht and a plane.
3  If the computers were working today, we would be able to send e-mails.
4  If I were you, I'd spend plenty of time preparing for the presentation.
5  If I stayed on in this company, I'd never become a manager.
6  If they arrive at 9.30 instead of 10, we'll be able to start the meeting early.

## 3 Conditionals (2)

**1**

| | | | | | | | |
|---|---|---|---|---|---|---|---|
| 1 | a Yes | 2 | a No | 3 | a Yes | 4 | a No |
| | b Yes | | b No | | b No | | b Yes |

**2**
1  hadn't been driving, wouldn't have skidded
2  would have made, hadn't been
3  would have spent, had stayed
4  would have happened, had taken
5  had not invested, would have kept

**3**
1  a would have been able
   b wouldn't have been able
2  a wouldn't be typing
   b would have saved
3  a would not have taken
   b would be

## 4 Future (1)

**1**  1 e   2 a   3 b   4 d   5 c

**2**  1 b   2 a   3 a   4 a   5 b

## 5 Future (2)

**1**  2

**2**  1 b   2 d   3 c   4 a

**3**  1 a   2 b

**4**
1  will have disappeared
2  will be using
3  is to introduce
4  will have become
5  will be choosing
6  will have launched, will be rolling in

## 6 Infinitive and gerund (1)

**1**
1  I apologise for being late.
2  She expects to get a positive response soon.
3  They are threatening to change supplier.
4  She claims to have the chairman's confidence.
5  I recommend trying again.
6  He didn't wish to be rude.
7  I don't mind working hard as long as …
8  My job involves making difficult decisions all the time.
9  I hope to see you soon.
10  She dreads going into work.
11  He refused to comment.
12  How can you justify spending so much on entertainment?

**2**
1  He was encouraged to apply for the job.
2  They are expecting the chief executive to resign.
3  She was instructed to report for work at 8 o'clock.
4  He can't prevent her from making a complaint.
5  The World Bank enables poor countries to borrow money for development projects.
6  They claimed to have reached their targets but they were lying.

## 7 Infinitive and gerund (2)

**1**

| | | | |
|---|---|---|---|
| 1 | to bring | 7 | talking, to listen |
| 2 | being | 8 | to have |
| 3 | meeting | 9 | doing |
| 4 | to switch | 10 | to help |
| 5 | leaving | 11 | to become |
| 6 | to sound | 12 | talking |

**2**
1 For the experiment to be valid, it is essential to record the data accurately.
2 If you haven't got much money, it can be advantageous to pay by monthly instalments.
3 As a start-up company in a competitive area, it is unlikely to make a profit in the short term.
4 Given the state of the traffic, we were right not to go by car.
5 I am very sorry to inform you that your services will no longer be required.

## 8 Modals and related verbs (1)

**1**
1 don't have to – f
2 can – c
3 can – h
4 must – n
5 should – g
6 must not – k
7 don't have to – m
8 must not – b
9 will have to – j
10 must not – d
11 can't – i
12 must – a
13 should – e
14 ought to – l

## 9 Modals and related verbs (2)

**1** 1 a  2 c  3 b  4 a  5 c  6 a

**2** 1 b  2 a  3 d  4 c

## 10 Nouns

**1**
| UNCOUNTABLE | COUNTABLE |
| --- | --- |
| traffic | vehicles |
| equipment | machines |
| insurance | policies |
| employment | jobs |
| travel | trips |
| progress | advances |
| advice | suggestions |
| legislation | laws |
| news | bulletins |

**2**
1 an advertisement
2 public transport, heavy traffic
3 some advice
4 some software
5 home, a headhunter

**3**
1 publicity campaign
2 exhibition stand
3 display materials
4 translation agency
5 exhibition staff
6 sales leads

## 11 Passive

**1**
1 be clarified
2 be made
3 be achieved
4 be obtained
5 is collected
6 analysed
7 does
8 is mapped out
9 be collected
10 be tested
11 be provided
12 be involved
13 has been installed
14 be taken
15 is checked

## 12 Past simple and present perfect

**1**
1 has been
2 played
3 changed
4 has made
5 sold
6 cost
7 mastered
8 drank
9 smoked
10 have been
11 has had to
12 has tried
13 used
14 argued
15 reached
16 did not do
17 received
18 has not lost

## 13 Past simple, past continuous and used to

**1**
1 rang
2 answered
3 were standing
4 didn't go
5 was talking
6 got
7 did you get
8 was working
9 met
10 was visiting
11 started
12 wasn't looking
13 made
14 came

**2**
1 He was having a meeting when there was a power cut.
2 His computer crashed when he was writing e-mails.
3 He was having lunch when he spilled his soup.
4 He was surfing the Web when his computer got a virus.
5 He was giving a presentation when he had a heart attack.

**3**
1 used to wear
2 dreamt, used to be
3 used to drive, went
4 were you talking, were
5 used to be, left

## 14 Phrasal verbs

**1**
1 ✓
2 ✗ What time did you get in this morning?
3 ✓
4 ✗ Did you remember to turn it off?
5 ✗ She's looking into the problem.
6 ✗ We carried out a full investigation.
7 ✗ I came across a very interesting article.
8 ✓
9 ✗ How does she put up with the noise?
10 ✓

**2** Sentences which do not need an object to complete them:
1, 3, 7, 8, 9
2 a  4 d  5 c  6 e  10 b

**3** 1 e  2 b  3 d  4 a  5 c

## 15 Present perfect simple and present perfect continuous

**1**
1 been trying, haven't found
2 has smoked
3 has been ringing
4 has done, has worked, has organised, has been, has directed
5 has given
6 have been reading
7 have been driving
8 has been behaving, has he been doing, has been talking, pacing, have seen, Have you talked
9 have worked, have been looking
10 have you read, have you been doing, have had, have made

## 16 *Present simple and present continuous*

**1**

| | | | |
|---|---|---|---|
| 1 | is making | 16 | think |
| 2 | work | 17 | 'm losing |
| 3 | do | 18 | 's beginning |
| 4 | 'm doing | 19 | 're not getting |
| 5 | take | 20 | understand |
| 6 | appear | 21 | hate |
| 7 | do you sleep | 22 | worries/is worrying |
| 8 | 'm not sleeping | 23 | need |
| 9 | 'm | 24 | eat/'re eating |
| 10 | suppose | 25 | have |
| 11 | is getting | 26 | recommend |
| 12 | 'm drinking | 27 | 'm trying |
| 13 | have | 28 | contain |
| 14 | live | 29 | need |
| 15 | weigh | 30 | 're getting on |

## 17 *Relative clauses*

**1**
- *a* who/that; a stockbroker
- *b* which/that; Netscape
- *c* where; Silicon Valley
- *d* whose; Charles B. Wang
- *e* which/that; a golden parachute
- *f* whose; fat cats
- *g* who/that; a day trader

**2**
1 Relay plc is a start-up company selling software for mobile phones.
2 The cable linking the two machines caught fire.
3 The building damaged during the storm will have to be pulled down.
4 All the people previously employed in manual jobs have been retrained.
5 The summit meeting taking place in Ottawa next week will make some important decisions.
6 The men being sent on this mission will receive danger money.

## 18 *Reported speech*

**1**
1 But earlier on you said that you'd just got back from New York.
2 But you just said that Sandra (had) left the company three weeks ago.
3 But you told me that you weren't thirsty.
4 But you said he claims that he doesn't know/he claims not to know how the money was spent.
5 But you assured me that you would refund my money if there were any problems.

**2** *1 d   2 b   3 f   4 a   5 e   6 c*

*Powerhouse* website

For links to over 100 websites with more information on many of the ideas, skills and people in this book, go to:

www.longman-elt.com/powerhouse